100 TOUGH
QUESTIONS

about

GOD AND THE BIBLE

100 TOUGH QUESTIONS

about

GOD AND THE BIBLE

STEPHEN M. MILLER

BETHANY HOUSE PUBLISHERS

a division of Baker Publishing Group
Minneapolis, Minnesota

© 2014 by Stephen M. Miller

Published by Bethany House Publishers
11400 Hampshire Avenue South
Bloomington, Minnesota 55438
www.bethanyhouse.com

Bethany House Publishers is a division of
Baker Publishing Group, Grand Rapids, Michigan

Printed in the United States of America

Library of Congress Cataloging-in-Publication Data

Miller, Stephen M.
    100 tough questions about God and the Bible / Stephen M. Miller.
       pages cm
    Summary: "Author answers difficult questions people have. Readers are offered popular viewpoints among biblical scholars and invited to draw their own conclusions" — Provided by publisher.
    ISBN 978-0-7642-1162-1 (pbk. : alk. paper)
    1. Bible—Miscellanea. I. Title. II. Title: One hundred tough questions about God and the Bible.
    BS612.M534 2014
    220.6′1—dc23   2013039793

Note: Other ancient writings that are quoted are the author's paraphrase into modern English.

Cover design by Dan Pitts

Author is represented by The Steve Laube Agency.

14 15 16 17 18 19 20   7 6 5 4 3 2 1

green
press
INITIATIVE

Contents

Introduction

Not being a preacher, I'm not inclined to preach at you.

So please don't expect me to tell you what to think.

I did graduate from seminary, but before that I was a news journalist—a newspaperman.

I love hard-hitting questions.

I love digging for answers.

I want the truth—even when it's contrary to what I think. Especially then.

What I don't want are:

- Clichés based on nothing in particular.
- Answers dodged because it's the safe thing to do.
- One-sided sermons about complex problems.

When I ask a question, I want an honest answer. Even if it's "I don't know."

I can handle that.

I think most Christians can, too. So can non-Christians and Bible newbies, especially those who are genuinely curious about God and the Bible but don't know what to make of it all.

Everyone respects openness and honesty.

Inside this book are some hard questions I've collected from Christians and non-Christians alike.

As for the answers, I won't be trying to sell you on one over the other.

Think of me as Switzerland.

Neutral.

I'm a journalist covering the Bible beat. I've tried to round up the best answers I can find and report them to you for your consideration.

I think you'll be surprised at some of the answers I found.

I was. And so was my editor.

A word of thanks

Books don't usually run credits like a movie does. But they should.

Books like this aren't a one-man show.

They're a three-ring circus.

Here are a few stars who deserve time in the spotlight:

Steve Laube, my agent. He pitched the book proposal to a select group of editors.

Tim Peterson, acquisitions editor. He caught the pitch.

Dan Pitts, Ellen Chalifoux, Nancy Renich, Dan Malda, and all the others at Bethany House who helped this book become reality.

God bless them. Every one.

Steve
Stephen M. Miller
StephenMillerBooks.com

1 What on earth do Christians mean when they say the Bible is "inspired by God"?

Did God:

- dictate it
- somehow mind meld his Spirit to the spirit of human writers
- or point out the general direction, and then let the writers run with it?

Yes. To all three.

Christians are that diverse in their opinions on the matter. They don't agree on how we got the Bible.

Many insist that God was so intimately involved in writing every word that the original manuscripts were error-free. "Inerrant" is the tech word Bible experts use.

Sadly, as far as we know at the moment, not one original manuscript survives. Not even a piece of one. So it's impossible to test inerrancy by fact-checking a manuscript for mistakes.

One mistake on an original manuscript is all it would take, it seems, to sink inerrancy—a bit like finding the corpse of Jesus would gut Christianity.

Other Christians argue that God played a less direct role in guiding the writers.

Despite their disagreements, both groups agree that God inspired the writers. To support their claims they turn first to the Bible:

- Prophets often introduced their messages by saying, "Listen to the word of the Lord" (Jeremiah 2:4).

- Jesus, debating Jewish scholars, quoted a line from Exodus and asked: "Haven't you read what God told you?" (Matthew 22:31).
- Preachers described their sermons as messages from God: "Paul said to Barnabas, 'Let's go back to every city where we spread the Lord's word'" (Acts 15:36).
- The most famous link between the Bible and God shows up in a letter Paul wrote to his friend Timothy, who was pastoring the church in Ephesus, a city in what is now Turkey:

> Every Scripture passage is inspired by God. All of them are useful for teaching, pointing out errors, correcting people, and training them for a life that has God's approval. They equip God's servants so that they are completely prepared to do good things.
>
> 2 Timothy 3:16–17

One problem with that quote.

Paul wasn't talking about our Bible.

He was talking about his: the Jewish Bible. Christians call it the Old Testament.

Paul probably had no clue, many scholars say, that within 300 years his letter to Timothy would find its way into the Holy Bible. As far as Paul was concerned, he may have been simply writing a letter to his friend. But Christians apparently saw in the letter's content evidence of God at work. So they made copies of it and circulated it among the churches, where Christians started reading it out loud in worship services.

Though most Christians agree God inspired Paul and the other Bible writers, few seem to know how he did it.

One exception: folks who lobby for dictation.

A minority among Christians, they draw some of their support from a phrase Paul used to describe Scripture in the quote above: "inspired by God." A more literal translation is "God-breathed."

This odd phrase comes from a Greek combo word that some guess Paul may have invented to explain what he meant by inspiration: *theo-pneustos*. *Theo* is God. *Pneustos* is related to the word we use in English to describe tools, like nail guns, powered by air: *pneumatic*.

Paul's word literally means "God air," or "God-breathed."

As far as Paul was concerned, Scripture is "God-breathed," which some say means that every word in the Bible is God-spoken, God-approved, God-powered.

Other Christians who don't buy into the dictation theory struggle to explain exactly how God inspired the Bible writers.

Some compare God to a muse who mystically inspires a painter or a poet. But most Christians argue that the Bible comes from a higher grade of inspiration—and a higher Source. One Bible writer put it this way: "No prophecy ever originated from humans. Instead, it was given by the Holy Spirit as humans spoke under God's direction" (2 Peter 1:21).

Here's the hard question: How do we know which writings were inspired by the Holy Spirit?

It's the hard question because:

• We don't know who wrote most of the books in the Bible.
• We don't know exactly how those books ended up in the Bible.

Could it be that some books don't belong there? Say, the Song of Songs or Esther—neither of which even mention God?

Some Bible experts say we don't need to worry about it.

That's because they say the same Holy Spirit who inspired the writers inspires the readers. The Spirit within us recognizes the Spirit within Scripture. That's why the first Christians latched onto certain stories of Jesus and letters about the faith when there were plenty of other stories and letters from which to choose.

That's also why, these experts contend, Jewish and Christian scholars centuries later gave their stamp of approval to writings that their communities of faith had already revered as sacred: the Old Testament (Jews and Christians) and the New Testament (Christians).

In ancient religious council meetings, some Bible experts say, it wasn't just a matter of scholars working through a slush pile of submissions and then applying their checklist to figure out which manuscripts should make the cut:

- written by a prophet or apostle or someone who knew them
- in sync with other Bible teachings
- widely accepted by people of faith as God's Word

Instead, the process began in house churches all over the Roman world. When they got letters from Paul and others, along with the Gospels about Jesus later, they read them in worship services. They found them so inspired and inspiring that they copied them and passed them along to others.

The decision about what to include in the New Testament actually started with a heretic: Marcion. Most church leaders didn't like the Bible he proposed.

Bible historians say that about a century after Jesus, in AD 140, Marcion put together a short collection of what he called the sacred writings, which he edited to fit his teachings that weren't especially orthodox; he rejected the God of the Old Testament.

His Bible included just one gospel, Luke, along with most of Paul's letters. That's about half of today's New Testament.

Church leaders quickly began listing the writings they considered sacred and inspired by God. These were writings that churches had already been reading in worship services almost from the time Paul and others had first written them.

We have twenty-seven books in our New Testament. The first time that list shows up anywhere, it comes in an Easter letter that a bishop of Rome sent out to his churches in AD 367. He was quoting African bishop Athanasius, who listed all twenty-seven, then added: "These are the fountains of salvation, and they who thirst may be satisfied with the living words they contain."

Thirty years later a council of church leaders agreed.

Many Bible experts say the Holy Spirit guided this process from start to finish. God's Spirit helped:

- writers present spiritual truth
- readers recognize the truth when they saw it
- church leaders sanction and organize the library of sacred books

Bible experts say Jesus predicted as much: "When the Spirit of Truth comes, he will guide you into the full truth" (John 16:13).

After Jesus returned to heaven, and the Spirit arrived "on the day of Pentecost" (Acts 2:1 NLT), another writer reported that Jesus' prediction had come true: "The Holy One has given you his Spirit, and all of you know the truth. So I am writing to you not because you don't know the truth but because you know the difference between truth and lies" (1 John 2:20–21 NLT).

Still, Christians don't agree on how involved God's Spirit was in the process of inspiring the writers.

Two more tech terms:

Plenary—the ideas were inspired, but writers often chose their own way of expressing those ideas—their own words.

For example, the prophet Nahum may have been inspired to predict the fall of the brutal Assyrian Empire, which was based out of Iraq. But he may have used his own words:

> "I am against you, Nineveh," declares the Lord of Armies. "I will lift up your dress over your face. I will show nations your naked body and kingdoms your disgrace. I will throw filth on you. I will make you look like a fool. I will make you a sight to be seen."
>
> Nahum 3:5–6

For some readers, a quote like that sounds more earthy than celestial.

Verbal—the words were inspired, too. Not just the ideas.

The Chicago Statement on Biblical Inerrancy, signed in 1978 by about 300 evangelical Bible scholars, explains it this way: "The whole of Scripture and all its parts, down to the very words of the original, were given by divine inspiration."

This doesn't necessarily mean God dictated the words. But it does mean he somehow got his own choice of words into the heads of the writers and onto scrolls.

Many don't buy into that particular theory.

Most do, however, agree on this: the Bible is a sacred collection of writings that contains messages from God to human beings.

Stories—some disturbing, but revealing.

Poetry—some raw, but insightful.

Advice—some hard to swallow, but worth digesting: "Love your enemies, and pray for those who persecute you" (Matthew 5:44).

It would be wonderful if Christians could agree on how we got the Bible—even better if any one of their theories made perfect, rational sense.

But many hear these ideas and say just the opposite. Too many holes in the theories. Not enough evidence presented. Too much faith required.

In the end, many Christians would agree that it takes faith to believe that God inspired the Bible.

It's a Holy Spirit thing, some would add. The Spirit who inspired the Bible is the Spirit who confirms it within the hearts and open minds of people searching for God.

Or as history quotes John Calvin (1509–1564), theological father of some Baptists and Presbyterians: "The testimony of the Spirit is more excellent than all reason."

2 We're supposed to believe that once upon a time people like Noah lived more than 900 years?

Imagine History 101 if folks today lived as long as some of those millennials in Bible times.

Skip books about the Crusades.

Forget PBS documentaries resurrecting those age-old battles with the help of cartoony, medieval etchings.

If people still lived as long as the Bible's record holder—Methuselah, age 969—call in the guest lecturers:

• Richard the Lionheart (1157–1199) speaking for Christians
• Saladin (1137/38–1193) defending the Muslim cause

Who in their right mind is going to believe that human beings used to live that long? The best we can do today—with a boost from modern medicine—is about 120 years.

Bible experts admit this is one tough problem to tackle. But they offer up a few theories.

Believe it, as is. Many Christians take the numbers literally. They also call attention to a pivotal moment in the Bible's story: the flood. That's when human lifespans suddenly dropped off.

Some Bible students theorize that the flood changed the earth's environment, perhaps releasing underground toxins that tripped a chemical switch in the human body. Or maybe the rain that got squeezed out of the clouds somehow diminished the earth's protection from the sun.

On the other hand, some say there may have been no physical change at all. God may have decided that humans no longer deserved to live that long.

When the Bible writer warned of the coming flood, he said humans had become evil. He quoted God saying, "My Spirit will not put up with humans for such a long time, for they are only mortal flesh. In the future, their normal lifespan will be no more than 120 years" (Genesis 6:3 NLT).

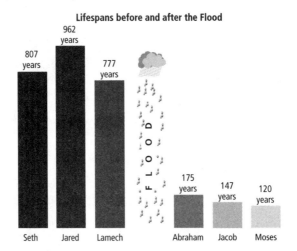

Lifespans before and after the Flood

Year = month. For Christians who can't warm up to a literal take on those huge numbers, one option is to interpret each year as a month—under a wild-guess theory that when ancients talked about a year they were talking about one cycle of the moon instead of the sun.

If we divide those huge numbers by 12, the lifespans are believable. Methuselah lived about 81 years instead of 969. Adam lived to age 77.

But that poses another problem: the age at which they fathered kids.

It seems a tad unbelievable that Adam fathered his third son, Seth, when he was still ten years old. It leaves us wondering how old he was when he fathered Cain and Abel. Five? That's how old Mahalalel would have been when he fathered his son—or age sixty-five, if we go for the literal take on the story.

It's exaggeration, to honor ancestors. Just as we honor our dead with glorified biographies and monuments, the ancients honored their larger-than-life ancestors with larger-than-life stats. That's another theory.

Many Jews in Bible times taught that God rewarded righteous people with prosperity and long life. "If you obey all the decrees and commands I am giving you today," one Bible writer said, quoting God, "all will be well with you and your children. . . . You will enjoy a long life" (Deuteronomy 4:40 NLT).

So, as the theory goes, Jews often portrayed their most ancient ancestors that way. Prosperous and nicely aged.

Jews weren't alone in that.

One clay document from the world's first known civilization—Sumer—did the same for their kings. The document is a four-sided prism from what is now Iraq. Scholars date it to about 1800 BC. That's some 400 years or more before Moses, who is traditionally credited with reporting the huge lifespans in the Bible book of Genesis.

If we take the Sumer prism literally, the first eight kings in their empire ruled for nearly a quarter of a million years: 241,200. The king with the shortest reign ruled 18,600 years.

These are kings, by the way, who ruled before what the Sumerians report as a great flood.

That's a big "Aha!" for Christians who take the Bible numbers literally. Huge lifespans before the flood show up in the Bible and in other ancient documents.

Christians who take the numbers as polite exaggerations, however, make much the same claim: Exaggeration was in style back then.

3 When Israel's high priest wanted to hear from God, he used some magical stones called Urim and Thummin, which gave him a yes or no answer. Isn't that a bit like flipping a coin?

Pretty much, except for the part about the "magical stones." Moses called them "sacred lots" (Deuteronomy 33:8 NLT).

No one knows what they looked like. But one guess is that they were stones painted with a light side and a dark side—as distinct as "heads" and "tails" on a coin. Some Bible experts say *Urim* may mean "light" since it sounds much like the Hebrew word for light: *or*. It's even more of a guess what *Thummin* means. One wild guess—a shot in the dark: "dark."

What's clear is how the Jews used them.

Starting with Aaron, Israel's first high priest, the stones rested in the high priest's vest pocket—"over Aaron's heart" (Exodus 28:30). The high priest was to use the stones "when direction from the Lord is needed . . . to determine his will" (Numbers 27:21 NLT). Apparently they would provide a yes or no answer.

Bible experts say that whenever they read in the Bible that the Jews "inquired of the Lord," they suspect the Jews were consulting the sacred lots.

Jews weren't the only people using lots to get advice from above. People throughout the ancient Middle East used lots. In the story of Jonah, sailors used them: "The crew cast lots to see which of them had offended the gods and caused the terrible storm. When they did this, the lots identified Jonah as the culprit" (Jonah 1:7 NLT).

It seems that the high priest's sacred lots weren't used as much after Israel's prophets came along. Prophets delivered God's messages to the people—in words far more impressive than a mere yes or no.

Yet the Jews never seemed to stop using lots entirely—even their own personal lots. They used lots to:

- divide Israel's land among the twelve tribes (Numbers 26:55)
- select Saul as their first king (1 Samuel 10:20–21)
- assign ministry jobs to temple workers (1 Chronicles 24:5)
- choose Matthias as the disciple to replace Judas (Acts 1:26)

Here's the question: Why link almighty God to something as flip as the flip of a coin?

The answer is simple: God's in charge. If he calls "heads," it's heads; if he calls "tails," it's tails. That's what the Jews seemed to believe.

As the Bible reports it, the technique worked. Sailors figured out that Jonah caused the storm. Joshua figured out that Achan's sin of looting valuables from Jericho had caused his men to lose a battle after God had ordered that the Jews take nothing from Jericho (Joshua 7).

Here's a follow-up question: If it worked then, why don't people of faith still toss lots to make big decisions? Why not use lots to pick a college, a career, a spouse? And instead of voting on a candidate for the church's next minister, how about flipping a coin?

Some Christians might say that's not a bad idea. Especially when it comes to picking a life partner. Nothing much to lose, it seems. As is, most studies seem to suggest that marriages have only about a 50/50 chance of survival.

On the other hand, most Christians would argue that today we have spiritual resources that the ancients didn't have.

We have the Bible, loaded with wise advice from godly men and women.

We have God's Spirit within us, guiding us in the decisions we make. That's an idea that many people outside Christianity would say is crazy. But most Christians say they believe it. They insist that Jesus predicted as much when he told his disciples he would be leaving soon:

> I will ask the Father, and he will give you another helper who will
> be with you forever. That helper is the Spirit of Truth. The world

cannot accept him, because it doesn't see or know him. You know him, because he lives with you and will be in you.

John 14:16–17

As the Bible reports it, God's Spirit arrived about a couple of months after Jesus' crucifixion. The Spirit's arrival fulfilled not only Jesus' prediction but a prediction from the prophet Joel: "God says, I will pour out my Spirit on everyone" (Acts 2:17).

4 The Bible says God gets jealous, but how is that not petty of him?

We've got our bad jealousy. Childish. Unjustified. Insane.
We see it when a guy can't believe his lady really loves the likes of him. So the dude smothers her, drives off imagined suitors, and accuses her of roving eyes and wandering affections.

We've got our good jealousy, too. Responsible. Justified. Rational.

We see it when a woman discovers that her husband is having an affair. If she weren't jealous, it would suggest she didn't care—that she didn't love her husband.

In the case of adultery, jealousy is what we expect to see in anyone who loves another and who is hurt by a lover's unfaithfulness.

That's God's brand of jealousy, as the Jewish writers reported it in their Bible, the Old Testament: "I, the Lord your God, am a jealous God" (Exodus 20:5 NLT).

Legit jealousy.

In a way, God married Israel. The two entered into a covenant agreement.

Israelite ancestors of today's Jewish people promised to devote themselves to God—to worship no gods but him. In return, God

26

promised to protect and bless them: "Carefully obey the Lord your God, and faithfully follow all his commands that I'm giving you today. If you do, the Lord your God will place you high above all the other nations in the world" (Deuteronomy 28:1).

Jews cheated on God.

Several prophets compared the busted relationship to adultery. Hosea went so far as to marry a prostitute who, it seems, would have children by other men. Hosea married her to "illustrate how Israel has acted like a prostitute by turning against the Lord and worshiping other gods" (Hosea 1:2 NLT).

It was a fair comparison, many Bible scholars say. Idolatry was serious stuff, sometimes including sex rituals and even child sacrifice. In the sex rituals, a worshiper would have sex with pagan priests and priestesses. The sex was intended to entertain and please a god.

If God didn't care that his people were getting lured into a cult like this, Jews and Christians argue, he'd be one lousy god.

When people worship fake gods—especially with rituals that hurt themselves and others—Jews and Christians say a jealous God makes perfect sense.

 5 The Song of Songs in the Bible is so sexually charged that it sounds like it needs "rated for a mature audience." What's it doing in the Holy Bible?

Consider this sacred sound bite, lyrics from what many Bible experts say was a wedding song: "Your figure is like a palm tree, and your breasts are like its clusters. . . . 'I will climb the palm tree and take hold of its fruit'" (Song of Songs 7:7–8).

Some Bible critics say that sounds more like a bar song than a hymn. It would make for a pretty mild-mannered bar song today. But Christians would have to admit, a song with lyrics like that would certainly liven up a worship service.

Jews and Christians alike have struggled over what to do with this book, sometimes called the Song of Solomon. They don't agree on what it's about, where it came from, or what on earth it's doing in the Holy Bible.

Guesses about the source: it's a collection of love songs, or wedding songs, or a single love song, or a musical for a wedding— perhaps one of what the Bible writers say was King Solomon's thousand weddings.

The style of writing—complete with garden metaphors to describe lovemaking—reads a lot like Egyptian love songs from about 3,000 years ago, when Solomon lived and loved. Both draw from nature when quoting lovers saying really nice things to each other. Really nice.

Yet some of those compliments sound anything but flattering:

- "Your nose is like a tower of Lebanon" (7:4 NRSV).
- "Your stomach is like a pile of wheat" (7:2 NCV).

The gent wasn't saying, "You have a schnoz like the Leaning Tower of Pisa and a gut you'd have to haul on a hay wagon."

He was saying his gal was one finely chiseled work of art. He described her from head to toe. Exquisitely shaped nose. Thin waist, nicely curved inward like a tied bundle of grain.

He moved on to the palm tree metaphor, vowing to shimmy up her trunk and fill his hands and mouth with her fruit.

That's the trouble with the book. Too sexy.

Some scholars about 2,000 years ago said they didn't want it in the Bible. They argued against it in council meetings. It wasn't only that the book sounds irreverent. It doesn't even mention God.

Nevertheless, the book made the cut.

Jews and Christians alike decided against treating the Song as letters between a couple of lovers juiced up on hormones. Instead, for all but the past 200 years, most Bible scholars have interpreted the Song as an allegory.

Jews said it represented God's love for his chosen people. Christians said it symbolized Christ's love for the church.

During the Middle Ages—from about the AD 400s to the 1500s— the Song of Songs actually became one of the most preached books in the Old Testament.

Even celibate monks climbed on board. St. Bernard of Clairvaux (1090–1153)—who had taken a "no-sex" vow—wrote eighty-six sermons on the first three chapters alone.

Christian preachers loved allegory back then. It gave them the creative freedom to take a word or a sentence in the Bible and imagine the unimaginable interpretation.

For St. Bernard:

- "Let him kiss me with the kisses of his mouth!" (Song of Songs 1:2 NRSV) is talking about "the mystical kiss from the mouth of Christ" (Sermon 3). The kiss of salvation.
- "My beloved is to me a bag of myrrh that lies between my breasts" (Songs of Songs 1:13 NRSV). These breasts belong to the bride, who's a symbol of the church. The fragrant myrrh refers to "the fragrance with which the church is perfumed in the conversion of one sinner" (Sermon 10).

Yeah, right.

Most Bible experts today don't agree with the monk.

They say the song is about a man and a woman expressing their deepest feelings of love in both words and sexual intimacy. It's about God-approved sex.

It's not a bar song, most Christians would argue, especially given the verses sung last:

Hold me close to your heart like the seal around your neck. Keep me close to yourself like the ring on your finger. My love for you

is so strong it won't let you go. Love is as powerful as death. . . .
Strong as the grave. Love is like a blazing fire. It burns like a mighty
flame. No amount of water can put it out. Rivers can't drown it.

Song of Songs 8:6–7 NIRV

There's nothing casual about this love. It's love for the long haul.
Most Christians today argue that this is a message worth keeping.

 6 God said King Hezekiah would die of an illness, but a few minutes later said he would let Hezekiah live another fifteen years. How can someone who knows everything change his mind like that?

God doesn't change his mind, most Bible experts say.
They're taking their cue from several Bible passages, including this one: "The Lord is the Eternal One of Israel. . . . He
is not a human being, so he does not change his mind" (1 Samuel
15:29 NCV).
Enter King Hezekiah, sick to death.
God sent the prophet Isaiah to tell the king: "Set your affairs
in order, for you are going to die. You will not recover from this
illness" (Isaiah 38:1 NLT).
Hezekiah broke into sobs and started praying.
Isaiah was walking out of the palace when God told him to
turn around and give the king a new and improved message: "God
heard your prayers and he's giving you fifteen more years" (see v. 5).
That sounds like God changed his mind.
There are other stories in the Bible that also seem to report
God doing a 180:

- **Creation do-over.** "The Lord saw how bad the people on earth were. . . . He was very sorry that he had made them" (Genesis 6:5–6 CEV). Up next: the flood.

- **King do-over.** "The Lord told Samuel, 'Saul has stopped obeying me, and I'm sorry that I made him king'" (1 Samuel 15:10–11 CEV). David would replace Saul as Israel's king.

- **On second thought.** After compelling the prophet Jonah to go to Nineveh, in what is now Iraq, and tell the people that their city would be destroyed in forty days, God didn't destroy the city. The people repented, and God forgave them (Jonah 3).

That last example is the clue, Bible experts say.

It's not God who's changing. It's the people who are changing.

All God is doing is changing his plans to accommodate the changed people. Many scholars would argue that God knew all along what would happen, but that he let the timeline unroll itself.

In Hezekiah's case, the theory is that something about Isaiah's sad announcement or the king's prayer changed Hezekiah. That change added fifteen years to the king's life.

Who knows, maybe the prayer threw a switch in the king's DNA. Various studies testing the effects of prayer on sick people have shown conflicting results. A 2001 study published in the *Journal of Reproductive Medicine* reported that infertile women were twice as likely to get pregnant if people prayed for them. But a 2005 study at Duke University said prayer didn't help high-risk heart patients. So as far as science is concerned, the jury's still out on the effects of prayer.

In cases of God being "sorry" he made humans or "sorry" he crowned Saul king, scholars say that's just a way of expressing God's feeling of sadness—using terms humans can relate to.

The Hebrew word that can be translated as "sorry" or "grieved" is more about sadness than change. It's a bit like the heavy sigh of a father who has a rebellious son—and who just got a call from the police. The father knew the call would come someday, but that didn't make it hurt any less.

31

Some Bible experts don't try to defend the Bible's choice of words. Instead, they embrace the mystery of God. They say the Bible writers were simply trying to explain what was going on as best they knew how—but that their know-how was limited. It was limited because they were only human.

 7 How could Mary have been a pregnant virgin 2,000 years before in vitro fertilization?

It was tougher to believe in pregnant virgins before humans figured out how to get the job done, thanks to science.

With in vitro fertilization and artificial insemination, pregnant virgins are quite the possibility.

That leaves some Christians asking why it's so tough to believe that God could accomplish 2,000 years ago what humans can do today.

Even so, not all Christians say they believe what the gospels of Matthew and Luke report about Mary's pregnancy: "While she was still a virgin, she became pregnant through the power of the Holy Spirit" (Matthew 1:18 NLT).

Some Christians say they doubt this part of the story not just because the gospels of Mark and John skip it; those gospels skip everything that has anything to do with Jesus' birth and childhood. Some Christians say they doubt the virgin birth for other reasons, too:

• Matthew and Luke never mention it again, and it could be deleted without affecting anything else in their stories—almost as though it got edited in.

- Apart from Mary's song of praise to God in Luke, Jesus' family never mentioned it.
- No one else in the Bible mentioned it.

Christian scholars didn't seem to start doubting the story until recent centuries. That's when they began finding other ancient stories of virgin births.

Scholars also discovered that many Christians in the early centuries seemed to express great enthusiasm for virginity. Many believers said it was best not to marry, as though celibacy was the better path in life.

For reasons like these, some Bible scholars say the Bible story about Mary's virgin pregnancy is an add-on, perhaps after virginity became popular. If they're right, the virgin birth is a mythical embellishment, not a fact of history.

Those scholars, however, are out of sync with the long haul of tradition, others argue.

The virgin birth shows up in the earliest Christian writings outside the Bible: the teachings of major church leaders in the AD 100s, including Irenaeus, Justin Martyr, and Ignatius of Antioch. The virgin birth is also written into the early church creeds, such as the Apostle's Creed: "conceived by the Holy Spirit, born of the Virgin Mary."

That's a creed that people in many churches today recite during worship services to remind them of the basic teachings of Christianity.

Perhaps the key argument for the virgin birth is creation itself, some scholars say. If God can create something from nothing, why should it be impossible for him to create a baby in a uterus? God does miracles. Creation is the proof. While a minority of Christians say they can take or leave the virgin birth—that it's not necessary to their faith—many Christians, if not most, say that believing in the virgin birth doesn't seem like a huge leap of faith.

8 Why should anyone believe that a star led the wise men to Bethlehem when stars don't move like that?

Miracles happen.

That's probably the most honest answer Christians could give to the question about how wise men from somewhere east of Israel—perhaps Iran or Iraq—managed to track down young Jesus, whom they considered the future king of the Jews.

The story shows up in just one book of the Bible: "After Jesus' birth wise men from the east arrived in Jerusalem. They asked, 'Where is the one who was born to be the king of the Jews? We saw his star rising and have come to worship him'" (Matthew 2:1–2).

The wise men were magi—possibly astrologers who studied the movement of stars and planets, looking for signs about the future.

Magi often advised kings, especially when the rulers had to make important decisions, such as whether or not to go to war.

The Bible doesn't say how many wise men there were. Scholars say the idea that there were three probably comes from the three gifts they gave Jesus: gold, frankincense, myrrh.

Scholars offer several theories about naturally occurring events that may have produced the Bethlehem star. But not one tracks perfectly with the Bible story.

The Bible and Roman history offer a few hints, at least about the timing of the star.

Whatever the star was, it had to appear sometime before King Herod the Great died in 4 BC. Herod was the Rome-appointed king of the Jews when the wise men arrived in Jerusalem. The visitors asked Herod where they could find Israel's newborn, future king—as though Herod may have just become a daddy.

He had not.

And paranoid as he was, he had already executed two of his sons because he feared they were plotting a coup. He would kill a third son later.

There's another hint about the timing. The wise men apparently told Herod they first saw the star two years earlier. Herod "sent soldiers to kill all the boys in and around Bethlehem who were two years old and under, based on the wise men's report of the star's first appearance" (Matthew 2:16 NLT).

The star may have appeared in 6 BC—give or take a year or two. We need that "give or take" because the Bible doesn't say if Herod died shortly after he killed all those baby boys.

Three theories about the star

Supernova, 5 BC. Chinese stargazers described something that sounds like an exploding star. They reported seeing it during March and April in 5 BC.

Glitch: Romans studied the stars, too. No one has yet turned up any reports from them about a supernova in their corner of the world at the time.

Halley's Comet, 12 BC. A church leader named Origen (about AD 182–254) was the first Christian known to speculate about what the star was:

"We think that the star which appeared in the east was a new star and not like any of the ordinary ones. . . . It is to be classed with the comets which occasionally occur."

Halley's Comet appeared in 12 BC.

Glitch: That's beyond the range of Jesus' birth, so say most Bible experts. Most mark his birthday no earlier than 7 BC.

Alignment of planets, 7 BC. This is currently the most popular theory among Christians looking for an explanation that sounds reasonably intelligent.

The planets Jupiter and Saturn lined up beside each other—and beside the Pisces constellation. Seeing this, Magi studying the stars would have added one plus one plus one—and come up with three.

- *Jupiter represented kings.* That's because this huge planet was named after the Roman king of gods, known to Greeks as Zeus.
- *Saturn represented Jews.* That's because Jews worshiped on Saturday, the day named after the god Saturn. Roman historian Tacitus (AD 56–117) confirmed this, saying the god Saturn protected the Jews because they worshiped on the day that honored him. Records of Babylonian stargazers from what is now Iraq also report the link between Jews and Saturn.
- *Pisces represented Israel.* Pisces means "fish." It represented the land beside the Great Sea, known today as the Mediterranean. This would have included the Jewish homeland.

As the theory goes, the wise men would have known that Jews were anticipating the imminent appearance of the Messiah—a king from David's family. Jews expected the Messiah would free them from their Roman occupiers and restore Israel's independence and glory. Writings found in the famous Dead Sea Scrolls confirm that many Jews at that time obsessed about this.

The wise men would have known this, scholars say, because Jews lived scattered throughout the Middle East. So the magi would have concluded that the unusual alignment of Jupiter and Saturn beside the Pisces constellation meant that they should look for a king (Jupiter) among the Jews (Saturn), in Israel (Pisces constellation).

They set off. Not following a star. But heading in the general direction that the signs in the sky suggested.

That would explain why they went to Jerusalem, capital of the Jewish homeland, and asked to see the newborn king. It was the logical place to go. Only after King Herod consulted with his Bible experts did the wise men discover they needed to continue their journey to Bethlehem, six miles (10 km) south. Herod's scholars said the prophet Micah had predicted the Messiah would come from "Bethlehem in Judea" (Matthew 2:5).

Glitch. After the wise men left Jerusalem, "the star they had seen rising led them until it stopped over the place where the child was. They were overwhelmed with joy to see the star" (Matthew 2:9–10). This glitch applies to all the theories involving naturally occurring events. Stars don't move like lights on a flying airplane. And even if they did, they wouldn't turn off and on along the way. Some scholars say they wonder if this part of the story got miscopied or perhaps embellished by an excited editor.

Angelic being of light. There's one theory that tracks perfectly with the Bible. Unfortunately, as far as many people are concerned, that particular theory makes Christians look like they've gone off their medication.

The star was a being of light.

So say many Christians who take Matthew's story literally.

This light, some Christians explain, might have been something like the pillar of light that led Moses and the Jews out of Egypt: "The Lord went ahead of them. He guided them during the day with a pillar of cloud, and he provided light at night with a pillar of fire" (Exodus 13:21 NLT).

Glitch. Professional stargazers would have known the difference between a star and a being of light, or perhaps a pillar of light—unless the light was flying at a higher altitude than the one that led Moses and the Jews.

9 Since Jesus told people to turn the other cheek, why aren't more Christians pacifists?

Christians were pacifists for the first 300 years of Christianity. Most church history scholars agree on that much.

What turned peace-loving Christians into fighters?

A surprise gift: political power, wrapped in royal robes.

Roman Emperor Constantine—leader of the world's most powerful empire—declared himself a Christian. He backed it up in AD 313 with the Edict of Milan, ordering people throughout the empire to stop bullying Christians.

Suddenly, the previously outlawed Christian religion became Rome's preferred religion. Powerless one year. Packing political wallop the next.

Christians quickly learned to throw a punch.

Some of their leading theologians argued that a Christian empire needs to protect its people.

Why Christians were pacifists

Early church leaders preached love, not war:

> We no longer arm ourselves to fight a nation. We don't study the art of war, either. We are soldiers of peace, led by our commander: Jesus.
>
> Origen (about 185–254), *Against Celsus*

> When Christ disarmed Peter he disarmed every soldier.
>
> Tertullian (about 160–220)

Early church rule books said the same thing.

- Christians were forbidden to join the army.
- Soldiers converted while in the army could continue to serve, but not fight.
- Officers converted while in the army had to resign.

Apostolic Tradition, AD 200s

Pacifists used a literal take on the New Testament teachings of Jesus as ammunition for their argument—just as pacifist Christians do today.

- "Do not resist an evildoer. But if anyone strikes you on the right cheek, turn the other also" (Matthew 5:39 NRSV).

    Alternate Christian approach: "We will rid the world of the evil-doers." (President George W. Bush, in a speech on September 16, 2001, after the 9/11 terrorists attacks)

- "Love your enemies" (Matthew 5:44).

    Alternate Christian approach: Google "Crusades" (Christians vs. Muslims) or "Spanish Inquisition" (Christians vs. Jews and Muslims).

- "Do to others whatever you would like them to do to you" (Matthew 7:12 NLT).

    Alternate Christian approach: German minister Dietrich Bonhoeffer took part in a plot to assassinate Hitler. Bonhoeffer failed. He was executed. Many Christians today praise him for making the ultimate sacrifice.

The apostle Paul offers up a few rounds of ammo, too, some pacifist Christians say: "This is not a wrestling match against a human opponent. We are wrestling with rulers, authorities, the powers who govern this world of darkness, and spiritual forces that control evil in the heavenly world" (Ephesians 6:12).

Paul then draws a picture from the battle gear of Roman soldiers—as though he's trying to illustrate the superiority of the spiritual weapons Christians need to fight the real battles:

- belt of truth
- body armor of righteousness
- shoes of peace
- shield of faith
- helmet of salvation
- sword of God's Word

These spiritual weapons are more effective than any state-of-the-art weaponry that humans can come up with, pacifists say. These weapons are, after all, what Christians used to conquer the Roman Empire.

But they needed one other weapon, too: patience. Enough to endure 300 years of persecution—including occasional stretches of martyrdom.

Why some Christians fight

One of the first Christian scholars on record to argue against pacifism was one of the most famous theologians of all: an African bishop, Augustine (AD 354–430).

He invented the "just war" theory, some historians say. Augustine argued that there are times when war is justified—when it's conducted for the good of everyone.

Martin Luther (1483–1546), founder of the Protestant movement, agreed. But instead of preaching "just war," he talked about the reality of two kingdoms. In Christ's spiritual kingdom, there's nothing but peace. But outside that perfect world—in our world—war is sometimes God's way of restoring order.

To Luther's way of thinking, tyrants left unchecked will reign over a status quo of injustice: starvation, homelessness, sick people left untreated, legal systems favoring the rich, laws written by the rich and powerful for the rich and powerful, minorities targeted for discrimination, or worse. Luther would have argued that Christians need to take a stand against that.

History's best illustration of what Augustine and Luther preached: Hitler.

German minister Dietrich Bonhoeffer decided that the most loving thing he could do for Germany—as well as for Germany's enemies—was to turn Hitler into a Rorschach blot on a wall.

Christians who admire Bonhoeffer, and who agree that war can be the best of rotten options, criticize pacifists—sometimes with harsh words, calling them what amounts to biblically ignorant, naïve, yellow-bellied sapsuckers.

Locked and loaded, survivalist Christians, anticipating some kind of global apocalypse, remind their peace-loving brothers and sisters that two-thirds of the Bible is the Old Testament. And it's full of holy war—the justice side of God's love.

As Bible writers reported it, God sometimes ordered Jews to wipe out their enemies: "Leave nothing alive in the cities of the land the Lord your God is giving you. Completely destroy these people: the Hittites, Amorites, Canaanites, Perizzites, Hivites, and Jebusites, as the Lord your God has commanded" (Deuteronomy 20:16–17 NCV).

God sometimes sent enemies to wipe out the Jews, too: "I will scatter you among the nations. War will follow you. Your country will be in ruins. Your cities will be deserted" (Leviticus 26:33).

In the name of God, there was blood.

Pacifist Christians respond with questions:

1. Did God really order all of those wars, or were the Bible writers—usually anonymous—simply jumping to that conclusion when they wrote Israel's history?
2. When has God issued a call to arms in modern times? Are wars today the will of God, or the will of a tiny few sitting behind big desks—national leaders who will never find themselves

41

or their children within the 2,000-meter range of a battlefield sniper?

Christians who defend the just war counterattack. They remind pacifist believers that when Jesus came face-to-face with a Roman officer, he commended the warrior. Instead of telling the soldier to "Go and kill no more," Jesus said, "I haven't found faith as great as this in anyone in Israel" (Matthew 8:10). Period.

These Christians add, "What about the survival instinct? Why did God give us a survival instinct if he didn't expect us to use it?"

Pacifists reply, "Why would Jesus tell us to love others as much as we love ourselves and to count on living forever if he didn't expect us to believe it?"

Early Christians believed it, if church historians got their homework right. Some Christians today believe it, too. But many, if not most, seem to favor a little life insurance on the side.

10 If Jesus was so great, you'd think Roman or Jewish history writers of his own time would have written about him. Did they?

They did. Jesus shows up in Roman and Jewish history books written in his own century.

It's a common mistake people make—thinking Jesus didn't exist, that he was just another myth, like the Greek god Zeus or heroes such as Hercules and Achilles.

Jesus was born somewhere around 6–4 BC and he died somewhere around AD 30–33; scholars debate the exact dates.

Here are what a few Romans had to say about Jesus.

Disciples say he rose again

There was a wise man called Jesus, and his conduct was good. . . .
Pilate condemned him to be crucified. . . . His disciples didn't give
up on their loyalty to him. They reported that he appeared to them
three days after his crucifixion, and that he was alive.

Josephus (about AD 37–101), *Antiquities of the Jews*

That's the most famous reference to Jesus outside the Bible.
The writer, Josephus, was born just a few years after Jesus died.
A Jew as well as a citizen of Rome, Josephus included Jesus in his
many-volume history of the Jews. Josephus wrote this history to
help Romans better appreciate his race, since Romans had been
occupying the Jewish homeland for more than a century.

Ancient copies of Josephus's reference to Jesus suggest that
Christians edited some of them. One version makes it sound as
though Josephus believed Jesus rose from the dead. The version
above has Josephus simply reporting that Jesus' disciples believed it.

Pilate executed Christ

Christ suffered the ultimate penalty at the hands of procurator
Pontius Pilate when Tiberius was emperor of Rome.

Tacitus (about AD 56–120), *Annals of Imperial Rome*

Tacitus was a Roman official, a respected public speaker, and
one of Rome's greatest historians. *Annals* is a multivolume history of Rome covering more than half a century, from AD 14–68,
spanning the reigns of emperors Tiberius to Nero.

Some Christians cursed Christ

I forced those accused of being Christians to deny the charge and to
prove it. I had them pray to the gods a prayer I dictated. And I had

them offer wine and incense to your image and to curse Christ. It is said that true Christians could never be forced to do any of these. Others named by an informer said they had been Christians—some three years ago, some as much as 25 years ago. But they said they were not Christian any longer. They all worshiped your image and the statues of the gods. They also cursed Christ.

Pliny the Younger (about AD 61–113),
letter to Emperor Trajan

Pliny was a Roman writer and administrator who left a library of letters that offers insights into the public and private lives of Romans during the early years of the Christian movement. The excerpt above illustrates the technique he used to weed out followers of the outlawed Christian religion while he governed a Roman province in what is now Turkey, where the apostle Paul started many churches.

Christ the troublemaker

Because the Jews were making constant trouble at the instigation of Christ [Chrestus], Emperor Claudius expelled them from Rome.

Suetonius (about AD 69–122), *Lives of the Twelve Caesars*

Suetonius was a Roman historian. His reference to Claudius's evicting Jews from Rome seems to track with a report in the Bible:

Paul left Athens and went to the city of Corinth. In Corinth he met a Jewish man named Aquila and his wife Priscilla. Aquila had been born in Pontus, and they had recently come from Italy because Claudius had ordered all Jews to leave Rome.

Acts 18:1–2

11 Given what we know today from science, why do so many Christians say the universe was created in six days, a few thousand years ago?

Two out of three churchgoing folks seem to believe just that. So reports a Gallup poll taken in 2012. Almost half the country says they believe it, too: 46 percent.

This leaves many thinking souls wondering whatever happened to science classes.

But for many Christians, it's not a matter of science. It's a matter of faith in the Bible.

As these Christians—and Jews alike—read the story of creation in Genesis, they read it as history revealed by God himself. It's literal stuff, they insist. It's not poetry, not a metaphor, and certainly not a myth.

Some of these Christians apply science to this literal reading of the Bible—creation science, it's called.

They'll look at scientific evidence differently than secular scientists do.

Most geologists will say that fish fossils found on mountaintops confirm their theory that mountains were once flatlands that have been pushed up by eons of geological activity, especially along fault lines.

Creation science advocates, on the other hand, say the fossils confirm their theory that the flood in Noah's time covered the mountains, and in the process gave the face of the planet an extraordinary makeover—to the point of creating mountain ranges in a few months.

The vast majority of scientists, however, say creation science is more of a religion than a science. They say this because creation science starts with the presumption that the Bible's story about creation is a literal fact, while other scientists search for truth in facts revealed, tested, and confirmed by data they can measure.

Many Bible experts say they have no trouble accepting the general consensus of scientists around the world: the earth is 2.5 billion years old, and the universe is about 14 billion years old.

These Christians say they simply don't read the Genesis story as literal history. Instead, they read it as a story crafted to counter ancient Middle Eastern myths about gods creating the world. The Genesis writer, these scholars argue, wanted everyone to know that God created everything that exists.

Questioning the literal read of the Genesis story, these scholars point out problems like these:

- If God created plants on day three, how did they survive without the sun, which God didn't create until day four?
- Why should we interpret the six days of creation as six twenty-four-hour days when God didn't make the sun and moon—our tools for measuring twenty-four-hour days—until day four?
- What's wrong with interpreting the "days" of creation as long stretches of time when other Bible writers say that "One day with the Lord is like a thousand years, and a thousand years are like one day" (2 Peter 3:8, see also Psalm 90:4)?

On the flip side, Christians defending the Bible's literal history of creation say that questions like these underestimate the power of God.

For example, they would ask what's so hard to believe about God keeping plants alive without sunlight. He is, after all, the light of heaven's New Jerusalem: "The city doesn't need any sun or moon to give it light because the glory of God gave it light" (Revelation 21:23).

Other Christians would argue that we shouldn't be reading Revelation literally, either, since it's apocalyptic lit—a style of writing famous for its extreme symbolism.

12 Why do most Christians believe there was a global flood in the time of Noah when most geologists say otherwise?

Not all Bible experts say they believe Noah's flood covered the entire planet.

Many argue for a regional flood, in the Fertile Crescent river valley where civilization began: along the Tigris and Euphrates rivers in Iraq.

But those who argue for a worldwide flood ask: "Where do you see a regional flood in a passage like this?"

> The water covered even the highest mountains on the earth, rising more than twenty-two feet above the highest peaks. . . . God wiped out every living thing on the earth.
>
> Genesis 7:19–20, 23 NLT

Christians who take the flood story literally offer two main pieces of evidence.

Flood stories. You can find them all over the world, woven into the history of at least seventy cultures from one side of the planet to the other, including that of the American Indians, China, the South Pacific, and Ireland.

Greek and Roman children grew up listening to the story of Deucalion and Pyrrha, a couple who saved their children and an assortment of animals from a flood by herding them all into a big boat shaped like a box.

Middle Eastern kids, in what is now Iraq, heard a similar story. In the *Epic of Gilgamesh*, a man named Utnapishtim (call him U-Guy) saved his family in much the same way Noah did. He built a boat, waterproofed it with tar, loaded it with family and animals, survived the flood, and even released a dove as Noah did to make sure the water had receded enough to disembark.

Fossils. Fish fossils show up in sediment all over the world, high and low, though dead fish are normally recycled too quickly to form fossils. They're eaten or they disintegrate in the water. A worldwide flood that quickly receded, however, would explain the fossils. The fish were suddenly entombed in sediment from the receding water.

Many Christians who don't take the Bible story literally argue for a flood limited to the world that the ancients knew. Archaeologist Leonard Woolley (1880–1960) said he found sediment evidence of an ancient flood in about 3500 BC that decimated a stretch of land some 400 miles long and 100 miles wide in the Euphrates River Valley. He speculated that it was Noah's flood.

Christians who lobby for a regional flood ask questions such as:

- How could anyone know that Noah's flood covered the entire planet at a time when no one had a clue the planet was anything but flat?
- Where did enough water come from to cover Mount Everest, some five and a half miles high (over 8,850 meters)? Earth would need about triple the water we now have to float a boat that high.

Christians who say they believe in a worldwide flood reply: God knows. And in God we trust.

13 To seal the partnership contract between God and Abraham, God told Abraham to circumcise himself. How is cutting on the dotted line anything like signing on the dotted line?

God made an agreement with Abraham.

Abraham's part of the deal:

- "Live in my presence with integrity" (Genesis 17:1).
- "You and all your descendants have this continual responsibility. . . . You must cut off the flesh of your foreskin as a sign of the covenant between me and you. From generation to generation, every male child must be circumcised on the eighth day after his birth" (Genesis 17:9, 11–12 NLT).

God's part of the deal:

- "You will become the father of many nations" (Genesis 17:4).
- "I will give you many descendants. Many nations and kings will come from you" (Genesis 17:6).
- "I am also giving this land where you are living—all of Canaan—to you and your descendants as your permanent possession. And I will be your God" (Genesis 17: 8).

It's anyone's guess why God decided on circumcision as a way to remind the Jews that they had a contract with him. Bible writers seldom explain why God does what he does—presumably because they don't know.

A few guesses:

- **Daily reminder.** Every time a Jewish male made use of his plumbing, he was reminded of his covenant agreement with God.
- **Context clue.** The agreement guaranteed that God would make the people of the Jewish nation "as numerous as the stars in the sky and the grains of sand on the seashore" (Genesis 22:17). Cutting a reminder of the agreement onto the penis targeted the body part that would play a fairly important role in the process. Circumcision was painfully logical.
- **Holiness.** Jews were taught that by obeying God's laws, they could live holy lives—that their spirituality had the power to turn their physical lives holy. Putting the sign of the agreement with God on the lowly and usually hidden penis was a way of saying that even the most embarrassing part of the body could be used in a holy way. It also suggests that Jews should consider sexuality as sacred.
- **Health concerns.** It's easier to keep a circumcised penis clean. Recent medical studies have shown that circumcised men are less likely to pass along diseases such as HIV, herpes, and HPV, which can cause cervical cancer.

Jews weren't the only race of people circumcising themselves in the ancient Middle East. Egyptians did it. So did many nations in what is now Israel's neighboring Arab country of Jordan (then called Edom), Ammon, and Moab.

One famous exception: the Philistines. When Samson told his thoroughly Jewish parents that he planned to marry one of those gals, they were not pleased: "Do you have to go get a wife from the uncircumcised Philistines?" (Judges 14:3 THE MESSAGE).

14 Inconsistency alert: John 1:18 says, "No one has ever seen God," but that's not what other Bible writers say.

Up front, here's the short answer that many Bible experts give: People in the Bible who reportedly saw God didn't see the real God. They saw only a manifestation of him, God in the form of an angel, for example.

John wasn't the only one who said humans haven't seen God. God said it, too. When Moses asked to see God in his glory, God said, "You can't see my face, because no one may see me and live" (Exodus 33:20).

God did, however, let Moses see his back as he walked away.

Jacob saw God

Yet several centuries before Moses, Jacob wrestled a mysterious man all night, vowing not to let go until the man blessed him. At daybreak, after the man blessed him, Jacob offered his take on the mystery man's identity—the first of three clues that point to God:

Clue 1. "I have seen God face to face, but my life was saved" (Genesis 32:30).

Clue 2. Jacob named the place *Peniel*, Hebrew for "Face of God" (Genesis 32:30).

Clue 3. The mystery man gave Jacob a new name: *Israel*, which means "He Struggles with God" (Genesis 32:28).

About a thousand years later, a prophet identified Jacob's wrestling partner as God—in the form of an angel: "Jacob wrestled with the angel and won. . . . He asked for a blessing, and God spoke to us there" (Hosea 12:4 CEV).

Seventy Jews saw God

"Moses went up with Aaron, Nadab, Abihu, and 70 of Israel's leaders. They saw the God of Israel" (Exodus 24:9–10).

It's hard to say what exactly they saw. The writer says only this about what God looked like: "Under his feet was something like a pavement made out of sapphire" (Exodus 24:10).

Really? That's it?

Afraid so.

Some Bible experts say that sounds a bit like the short version of a vision the prophet Ezekiel would report seeing a thousand years later. He saw . . .

> . . . a throne made of sapphire. On the throne was a figure that looked like a human. Then I saw what he looked like from the waist up. He looked like glowing bronze with fire all around it. From the waist down, he looked like fire. A bright light surrounded him. The brightness all around him looked like a rainbow in the clouds. It was like the Lord's glory.
>
> Ezekiel 1:26–28

But even in this vision, there's no indication that he saw anything more than a glowing manifestation of God. And there's no hint that he saw God's face.

Many Bible scholars say that John's point in saying, "No one has ever seen God," was to introduce Jesus: "God's only Son, the one who is closest to the Father's heart, has made him known" (John 1:18).

In other words, we can see God in Jesus. Not God's celestial face, but his divine character.

15 God's law said that if a jealous husband merely suspected his wife of having an affair, he could force her into a trial by ordeal. That's what God calls justice?

It got worse, actually. At least as many people today read the story. Here's the extra helping of injustice: What was good for the goose wasn't good for the gander. Husbands suspected of adultery didn't have to endure anything, except perhaps an evil eye and a cold shoulder from their wives.

On the other hand, a wife suspected of adultery, "whether she was actually unfaithful or not" (Numbers 5:14), got marched off to the priest.

Here's what happened, as reported in Numbers 5:17–24:

- **Muddy the water.** "The priest will take holy water in a piece of pottery and put some dust from the floor of the tent into the water."
- **Loosen the hair.** "The priest will bring the woman into the Lord's presence and loosen her hair."
- **Hold the offering.** "In her hands he will put the offering used for a confession (that is, the grain offering brought because of the husband's jealousy)."
- **Hold the water.** "The priest will hold in his hands the bitter water that can bring a curse."
- **Speak the curse.** "The priest will say to her, 'If no other man has had sexual intercourse with you and you haven't been unfaithful to your husband, you're not guilty. This bitter water that can bring a curse will not harm you. If, in fact, you have been unfaithful and have had sexual intercourse with another

man, may the Lord make you an example for your people to see what happens when the curse of this oath comes true: The Lord will make your uterus drop and your stomach swell.'"

- **Agree to the curse.** "The woman will say, 'Amen, amen!'"
- **Get the curse in writing.** "The priest will write these curses on a scroll and wash them off into the bitter water."
- **Swallow.** "He will have the woman drink the bitter water that can bring the curse."

What happens next? That's the big question that Bible translators can't agree on.

Some Bible versions say that if she's guilty, and perhaps pregnant by her lover, "her abdomen will swell and her womb will miscarry" (Numbers 5:27 NIV). Some readers say that sounds like a priest-approved abortion.

Other versions suggest that the curse doesn't kill a fetus, but it prevents the woman from ever getting pregnant: "If the woman has been unfaithful, the water will immediately make her unable to have children" (CEV).

In either case, where's the justice in any of this? What good does this bizarre trial do?

Speculation is all we've got.

Here's one theory scholars offer: It was a man's world. Men ran the show. If a husband got crazy jealous, he might do crazy things: beat his wife, divorce her, or worse, chase her and the kids off without divorcing her. Under Jewish law, a woman was not free to marry until her husband wrote "a certificate of divorce" (Deuteronomy 24:1). In those days, without being able to remarry she would have little or no means to support herself. Unmarried women were treated a bit like children are today: not allowed to own land, run a business, or work for a living. They survived mainly by the charity of others, by becoming slaves, or by selling themselves as prostitutes.

The trial by ordeal—sometimes called the Test of the Bitter Water—was a comparatively painless alternative to what a jealous husband might otherwise do if he didn't have to obey this law.

16 If Joshua stopped the sun and moon with his battlefield prayer, as the Bible says he did, that would have halted the 1,070 mph rotation of the earth. So why didn't everyone get whiplash?

If ever there was a prayer request more ambitious than those of Jesus—who instantly stopped storms and raised the dead—this is it: "Sun, stand still over Gibeon, and moon, stand still over the valley of Aijalon!" (Joshua 10:12).

Go ahead. Tell the sun to chill.

That's what the Bible writer says Joshua did.

The result: "The sun stopped in the middle of the sky, and for nearly a day the sun was in no hurry to set" (Joshua 10:13).

Joshua prayed that prayer after leading his militia on an all-night march some twenty miles (32 km) or more up out of the Jordan River Valley, into the Judean hills of what is now the West Bank. Joshua's militia came to the rescue of the city of Gibeon, which had been surrounded by a coalition of five armies.

Plenty of Christians insist that stopping the sun and moon in the sky would have been no big deal for the Creator of the universe. So they take the story literally. Many Bible experts say that's probably the way the writer intended us to read it.

Other Christians raise a few questions from physics class:

- Wasn't it the earth's rotation that would have needed to stop, since that's what produces the illusion of the sun moving?
- How would the earth's sudden stop affect gravity?
- What about the atmosphere that rotates with the earth? Its momentum would keep it moving at a thousand miles an hour (1,600 km/h), creating a wind powerful enough to sweep the planet clean.

Christians who suspect that God worked within the laws of physics that he created look for other ways of understanding what happened.

Eclipse. One theory says the story grew out of a solar eclipse. And, apparently, got exaggerated. Solar eclipses don't last all day.

Poetry. Another theory says Joshua's prayer was reported as poetry, apparently quoted from an older, lost book: "Isn't this recorded in the Book of Jashar?" (Joshua 10:13). If so, we should probably give the writer a poetic license to drive. Yet a counterpoint is that the writer's commentary on the prayer isn't poetry. The writer said, "The sun stopped in the middle of the sky" (v. 13). On the other hand, many Bible experts say the writer wasn't a witness to the miracle. He was an editor who compiled all the ancient source material about a thousand years after Joshua's lifetime, when the Jews started pulling together all their most sacred writings.

Hailstorm. A more popular theory targets the Hebrew word for "stop." It's *damam*. It can mean "stop moving." But it can also mean "stop," as in stop shining.

If that's what Joshua was asking, perhaps he was worried that a day of fighting under a hot sun would quickly drain the energy out of his men, who were already tired from the all-night march up into the hills.

The sun did stop shining. Storm clouds rolled in.

Joshua's men attacked. And as their enemies fled, "the Lord threw huge hailstones on them. More died from the hailstones than from Israelite swords" (Joshua 10:11).

17 God made Eve from Adam's rib? Are you ribbing me?

Many Bible experts shake their heads over this story and admit they aren't sure how to explain it.

"The Lord God took out one of the man's ribs and closed up the flesh at that place. Then the Lord God formed a woman from the rib that he had taken from the man" (Genesis 2:21–22).

Among the many theories—none of which most scholars say rings the bell—there are three that show up most often.

It's a pun

The Bible writer adapted the ribbing from a Sumerian story, according to some scholars and to many critics of the Bible. Sumer was the first-known Middle Eastern civilization. It was based in what is now Iraq, homeland of Abraham, father of the Jews.

In the Sumerian language, "rib" is *ti*, pronounced *tee*. The word can also mean "to make alive."

In the Sumerian story, a god named Enki had an injured rib. A goddess created a healer called "the lady of the rib," or "the lady who makes alive." The Sumerian word for "rib" can go either way, which is why it's a pun.

The Bible writer, as the theory goes, crafted his story with the Sumerian story in mind. That's why he talked about the rib. And that's why he later said Eve "became the mother of every living person" (Genesis 3:20). Eve was "the lady who makes alive" all of humanity.

It's a handful of flesh and bone

This is the only place in the Bible that the Hebrew word for "rib" refers to a body part. Usually, the word refers to the side of a building or a room.

In other ancient Middle Eastern languages, such as Akkadian, the rib doesn't usually refer to just the bone, but to the rib cage or to the bone, muscle, and tendons of the rib cage.

Some commentators speculate that God didn't take just a bone from Adam, but a fistful of flesh and bone. That's why, they theorize, Adam called Eve "bone of my bones and flesh of my flesh" (Genesis 2:23).

It's poetry

We're not reading about a surgery, many Bible experts say.

Poetic flare is crafted into this story, even though it's written as prose.

"Bone of my bones and flesh of my flesh" is a phrase the ancients often used to describe their family. Eve had that close of a connection to Adam.

That's why the writer used the word *rib*—a word that throughout the Bible usually means "side." Eve would stand side by side with Adam, as his devoted partner.

To paraphrase how some Bible scholars have put it throughout the centuries:

> Eve didn't come from Adam's feet, to get walked on.
> She didn't come from his head, to top him.

She came from his side to be his equal, from under his arm to enjoy his protection, from near his heart to experience his love.

It's history

A lot of Christians, perhaps most, say they read the story as history. They argue that there's no reason not to.

For one, the writer reports the story as a real event and offers no hint that he's spinning some kind of parable, pun, or metaphor.

For another, these Christians argue, there's nothing in this story that God couldn't do.

18 Given that snakes don't say much these days, why do many Christians insist that a snake talked Eve into eating the forbidden fruit?

The snake was more clever than all the wild animals the Lord God had made. He asked the woman, 'Did God really say, "You must never eat the fruit of any tree in the garden"?'" (Genesis 3:1).

This is one devil of a snake, if some of the ancient Jewish and Christian commentators got it right.

Even the last book in the Bible calls the snake Satan: "That ancient snake, named Devil and Satan, the deceiver of the whole world" (Revelation 12:9).

Many Bible experts, however, say they aren't so sure that the writer of the first book, Genesis, thought of the snake as anything other than a creepy, crawly critter.

If he thought it was the devil, he didn't bother to mention it.
And to many, that would seem like a whopper of an "Oops."

Whatever the critter was, it could outtalk a parrot.

Some guess it walked, too. But that's just a presumption based
on the punishment God gave it: "You will crawl on your belly. You
will be the lowest of animals as long as you live" (Genesis 3:14).

For all we know, the snake may have been a snake in the grass
all along. Or it could have been a chameleon—which would have
been ironic, since many see the critter as Satan of a different color.

Instead of reading the story as literal history, some commentators argue that it's more likely that the Genesis writer saw the
low-down condition of snakes in his day and presumed they got
what they deserved—in a curse from God. So he wrote the snake
into the story.

That would make the snake story fiction, a bit like a parable—
using a pretend character to spin a story with a message.

The message?

Possibly this: Humans have themselves to blame for the world
of hurt they live in. That's not the world God wanted for them.
It's the world they chose because of their disobedience.

There are several reasons the writer may have picked on a snake.
Here are three ideas, some of which are pitched by scholars as well
as Bible critics.

Déjà vu

The snake in Genesis did pretty much the same as the snake in an
ancient story from Babylon, in what is now Iraq. In the *Epic of
Gilgamesh*, the hero was about to get a plant that would protect
him from death. A snake beat him to it—and ate it. The Bible's
story twists that plot. Eve ate the plant, compliments of the snake.
Eve's plant did the opposite of protecting her from death. It guaranteed her death.

Déjà vu all over again

In a Sumerian story from the earliest-known civilization, in what is now Iraq, a god named Ningishzida was represented as a snake. He was said to have ruled the underworld. Sound like Satan? Also, he offered a hero named Adapa the bread of life: immortality. The snake in Genesis promised Eve, "You'll be like God" (Genesis 3:5).

Wise guy

Many people in ancient times saw the snake as a symbol of wisdom, which is how the Genesis writer describes it: "more clever than all the wild animals" (Genesis 3:1).

In Egyptian art, we sometimes see a snake on the king's crown— a symbol of power and wisdom.

Bible experts disagree over whether or not to take the talking snake story as symbolic or literal.

Some say the Genesis writer was simply trying to explain his own world situation: why snakes crawled, why women hated snakes, why childbirth was so painful, and why it was hard to grow crops.

Others say they see a mingling of history and symbolism, all intended to explain humanity's broken relationship with God.

Still others insist that the writer was accurately reporting history, as inspired by God's Spirit—and that a talking snake is a talking snake, and we can debate it until our tails rattle, but it's still a talking snake.

19 Why do many Christians say the wine and bread of Communion actually turn into Jesus' blood and body?

Of all the rituals Christians perform, including marriage ceremonies and baptisms, there's one ritual that stands out as the most sacred of all—at least in the minds of many Christians.

It's the ritual of eating a piece of bread and drinking a sip of grape juice or wine.

This ritual goes by many names:

• Communion
• The Lord's Supper
• Eucharist
• Mass

It's so cherished because it's not a ritual that the disciples or other church leaders decided to create. It's the one ritual that Jesus himself established.

He set it up during his last meal with the disciples, the night of his arrest. Apparently anticipating his crucifixion the next morning,

Jesus took some bread in his hands and gave thanks for it. He broke the bread and handed it to his apostles. Then he said, "This is my body, which is given for you. Eat this as a way of remembering me!" After the meal he took another cup of wine in his hands. Then he said, "This is my blood. It is poured out for you."

Luke 22:19–20 CEV

After Jesus' resurrection and his return to heaven, the Christian movement embraced this Supper commemorating His sacrifice:

"We met on Sunday to worship and celebrate the Master's Supper" (Acts 20:7 THE MESSAGE).

Today, most Protestants would say that the bread and grape juice or wine that their ministers serve during the sacrament of Communion is just that: bread and juice. It simply represents the broken body and shed blood of Jesus. It's a metaphor.

Catholics and Orthodox Christians might do more than call that a mistake by Protestants. Some might call it a heresy.

They teach that the bread and juice morph into the actual body and blood of Jesus.

The Christian tech term for that: *transubstantiation*. In Greek, the international language of Jesus' day, the word was *metousiosis*, from which we get the word "metamorphosis."

There are two main reasons they teach that.

It's in the Bible

Catholics and Orthodox Christians insist that Jesus said, "This is my body and blood," not "This is a metaphor."

Early Christians believed it

Writing about a century after Jesus, in the early AD 100s, Bishop Ignatius of Antioch, Syria, wrote a letter to Christians in Smyrna, Turkey. He was warning them about an upstart heresy that said Jesus wasn't really human, but that he was a spirit who only pretended to be human.

"Stay away from heretics like this," he wrote. "They don't take Communion or pray because they said the bread is not really the flesh of our Savior Jesus Christ, who suffered for our sins."

Justin Martyr gave a ditto to that in about AD 150: "It's not common bread and drink that we receive, but just as Jesus was made flesh by the Word of God for our salvation, so likewise the food which is blessed by the prayer of his word . . . is the flesh and blood of Jesus who became flesh."

Christians took some heat in the early centuries because Romans accused them of cannibalism.

It's not in the Bible

Protestants teach that the bread and wine or juice are symbols. To make their case they, too, appeal to the Bible and tradition.

There's a fair amount of Communion going on in the New Testament. But there's no mention at all of first-generation Christians calling the bread and wine the actual body and blood of Jesus.

Instead, most Protestants say these early Christians considered the ritual a reenactment from the Last Supper.

Some twenty years after Jesus, Paul said this when he described the ritual to Christians in Corinth:

> What you must solemnly realize is that every time you eat this bread and every time you drink this cup, you reenact in your words and actions the death of the Master. You will be drawn back to this meal again and again until the Master returns.
>
> 1 Corinthians 11:26 THE MESSAGE

He called the elements "bread" and "drink," not the body and blood of Jesus.

The first church handbook skipped it

The church's first known manual—*Didache* (DID ah KAY; Greek: "teaching")—doesn't say a word about the bread and wine morphing into flesh and blood.

20 Wouldn't it seem more reasonable to believe that Jesus' disciples stole his body instead of believing that he rose from the dead and walked away?

Disciples stealing the body of Jesus? That's the oldest theory in The Book.

As the Bible tells it, Jewish leaders bribed the soldiers guarding the tomb: "They gave the soldiers a large amount of money and told them to say that Jesus' disciples had come at night and had stolen his body while they were sleeping" (Matthew 28:12–13).

Some wonder what the soldiers' comeback would have been if their commander had asked, "How could you know that if you were asleep?"

Here's one important fact: no resurrection, no Christianity. That's how vital the resurrection of Jesus is.

Finding the corpse of Jesus would gut the Christian religion.

The apostle Paul put it this way: "If Christ wasn't raised to life, our message is worthless, and so is your faith" (1 Corinthians 15:14 CEV).

When Christians make their case for the resurrection, they generally point to a couple pieces of evidence.

From cowards to martyrs

Even modern Jewish scholars say it's a fact of history that something dramatic changed the disciples.

Daniel Schwartz, professor of history at Hebrew University in Jerusalem, discussing the resurrection on the ABC News program *20/20*, said, "I think definitely something happened. I don't know how they [followers of Jesus] convinced themselves. But the historical fact is, you've got people who are convinced he was resurrected."

Before the resurrection—while Jesus was being crucified and later while he lay dead in a tomb—most of the disciples apparently hid in a locked house. That may be where they stayed from Friday until Sunday, when Jesus showed up—inside the house while the door was still locked.

> The disciples were afraid of the Jewish leaders, and on the evening of that same Sunday they locked themselves in a room. Suddenly, Jesus appeared in the middle of the group. He greeted them and showed them his hands and his side. When the disciples saw the Lord, they became very happy.
>
> John 20:19–20 CEV

As the New Testament writers and early church leaders tell it, the disciples were never the same after that. They believed in life after death so much that they practiced what they preached. Most died as martyrs.

The Bible reports the execution of only James, the brother of John: "King Herod devoted his attention to mistreating certain members of the church. He had James, the brother of John, executed" (Acts 12:1–2).

But early church leaders in the AD 100s wrote about the martyrdom of most of the other disciples, too—by crucifixion, ax, and spear.

Bartholomew's execution was outsourced to India, where he reportedly was skinned alive and beheaded.

Resurrection in a Roman history book

It's not that Roman history reports the resurrection as a fact. But it does report the disciples' belief in it as a fact.

There was a wise man who was called Jesus, and his conduct was good. . . . Pilate condemned him to be crucified. . . . His disciples didn't abandon their loyalty to him. They reported that he appeared to them three days after his crucifixion, and that he was alive.

Josephus (about AD 37–101), Jewish historian and Roman citizen, *Antiquities of the Jews*

After the resurrection, the Bible says Jesus spent forty days on the planet. The apostle Paul said:

He appeared to the twelve apostles. Then he appeared to more than 500 believers at one time. (Most of these people are still living, but some have died.) Next he appeared to James. Then he appeared to all the apostles. Last of all, he also appeared to me.

1 Corinthians 15:5–8

It's anyone's guess why Jesus didn't go back to the Jerusalem temple and flaunt his heartbeat to the Jews who had arranged to stop it. Perhaps he thought it wouldn't have changed their minds—and that they'd simply decide to kill him again, as they decided to do with Lazarus.

Raised from the dead, "Lazarus was the reason why many people were leaving the Jews and believing in Jesus" (John 12:11).

What do you do with a dead man who won't stay dead?

Try, try again: "The chief priests planned to kill Lazarus" (John 12:10).

Perhaps Jesus figured that dying once and rising from the dead would be enough to convince the open-minded—but that the Jewish leaders were anything but open-minded.

21 How on earth could the Red Sea have parted so Moses and the Jews could escape from the Egyptian army?

The Red Sea has not parted lately—or ever, as far as anyone reading a history book can tell.

Stories like the one in the Bible haven't shown up in Egyptian history. If the Red Sea ever parted for them, you'd think they'd have written about it.

But the Red Sea may not have been the body of water that parted for Moses and the Jewish refugees when they fled Egypt during the Exodus.

Many versions of the Bible identify the body of water as the Red Sea—but with an asterisk: "God led the people around by the desert road toward the Red Sea*" (Exodus 13:18 NIV). The asterisk often reads something like this: "Or *the Sea of Reeds.*"

In the original language of the Old Testament—Hebrew—the words are *yam sup.*

The first known Bible translators, creating a Greek edition more than 100 years before Jesus, translated *yam sup* as "Red Sea." But most Bible experts today agree that was just a guess—and possibly not the best guess.

The Jewish refugees left the Egyptian town of Rameses in northern Egypt. There are several reed-framed lakes between Rameses and the Red Sea.

Other contenders for the Sea of Reeds: Lake Timseh, Great Bitter Lake, and Little Bitter Lake. The Jews would have passed by all of these on their way to the Red Sea.

However, if the first Jewish Bible translators got their guess right—that *yam sup* meant "Red Sea"—there are some scientific theories and some history that scholars say might help explain what happened.

In two separate studies, scientists specializing in meteorology and oceanography concluded that a strong, sustained wind could push back the beachfront water of the Red Sea's narrow Gulf of Suez—mimicking a low tide that extends the beach by about a mile (1.6 km). Then when the wind stopped, the water would rush back within half an hour, and up to ten feet (three meters) deep.

That sounds a lot like what the Bible described: "All that night the Lord pushed back the sea with a strong east wind and turned the sea into dry ground" (Exodus 14:21).

It would also help explain why Napoleon nearly drowned while riding his horse on the Red Sea's beach.

Napoleon invaded Egypt in 1799. And as he rode along the beachfront, the water rushed back to shore, like high tide running on fast-forward. A French report says Napoleon's expert horsemanship saved him. An Egyptian report said he fell off his horse and had to be dragged out of the water.

If this pushback of the oceanfront is what happened to Moses and the Jewish refugees, it still doesn't seem to track perfectly with the Bible's report:

"The water divided, and the Israelites went through the middle of the sea on dry ground. The water stood like a wall on their right and on their left" (Exodus 14:21–22).

At best, given this theory, the Jews might have had pools of water on their left and right as they walked across a sandbar or a reef. But no walls of water.

When the Egyptian chariot corps tried to follow them, they may have experienced what Napoleon did: "The water flowed back and covered Pharaoh's entire army, as well as the chariots and the cavalry that had followed Israel into the sea" (Exodus 14:28).

Many Christians read the story literally and say that whatever body of water the Jews crossed, God blew a path through the water for them—just as the Bible says.

For many, creation itself is the compelling evidence to support the facts of the story. Any God powerful enough to create the sprawling universe could easily send a windstorm to blow a path through something as comparatively tiny as the Red Sea.

Another option might feature a combo package of science, history, and exaggeration. Perhaps, some would say, the scientific theories explain what happened. And a touch of exaggeration might explain the "walls of water."

However, many Christians, if not most, would take unkindly to someone arguing that the Bible writer exaggerated such a key event in Jewish history.

22 Fire and brimstone destroyed the cities of Sodom and Gomorrah—and Lot's wife turned into a pillar of salt? Evidence?

Twin sin cities Sodom and Gomorrah got themselves scorched off the planet, as the Bible tells it.

"The Lord made burning sulfur and fire rain out of heaven on Sodom and Gomorrah. He destroyed those cities, the whole plain, all who lived in the cities. . . . Lot's wife looked back and turned into a column of salt" (Genesis 19:24–26).

What kind of rain could do that?

Not acid rain.

Sure, it's laced with corrosive chemicals such as sulfur dioxide. And these chemicals—which belch out of smokestacks and volcanoes, and can waft up from swamplands—are strong enough to rust steel and erode stone.

But no one would describe acid rain as "sulfur and fire." And acid rain doesn't wipe out entire cities. At least not yet.

Maybe it wasn't rain at all, some Bible experts speculate. Maybe it was the fallout of what amounts to a natural gas explosion in a chemical factory.

That's the most popular theory about what happened to Sodom, Gomorrah, and their neighboring villages.

There are several intriguing variations on that theory. Most put the villages in or near what is now the southern shallows of the Dead Sea. That's an area rich in explosive chemicals: natural gas, sulfur, potassium, along with more than enough salt to spray a hot crust on Lot's wife if she lingered near the blast radius. An Israeli mining company called Dead Sea Works harvests and processes chemicals from the water. Especially potash, which is loaded with potassium and sold as fertilizer.

Snap, crackle, and pop theory

An earthquake snapped open pockets of natural gas, according to this theory. Add flames from crackling campfires or village lamps and you get a big pop.

A blazing spray of superheated sulfur and salt killed everything beneath its umbrella.

Think Mount Vesuvius on a smaller scale. In AD 79 the Vesuvius eruption took out Pompeii. Residents died instantly, as soon as the searing ash collapsed on them. Archaeologists have recreated their shapes by injecting plaster into the holes inside the petrified ash.

Surfing turf theory

Ditto the snap, crackle, pop—but add a slide into the sea.

If the villages were built on sand beside the sea, an earthquake could have loosened the ground just long enough for gravity to pull the villages down the beachside slope and into the water.

That's a theory suggested by geologist Graham H. Harris and reported in the *Quarterly Journal of Engineering Geology and Hydrogeology*, November 1995.

Fire and flood

Again, ditto snap, crackle, pop. But add a flash flood afterward, erasing the villages.

This theory puts the villages on a plain inside what is now the southern Dead Sea shallows. As this theory goes, the earthquake dropped the populated plain enough to allow the Dead Sea water to rush in from the north—almost doubling the size of the sea.

It was a miracle

There are other theories, less popular at the moment.

Such as the theory that some ancient writer made up the story because he heard a legend about cities in the region burning, and he presumed it was because God was punishing them—since God's the boss of his creation.

Many Christians have never heard of any of these theories.

And some wouldn't like them if they heard them.

For many believers, if not most, God did a supernatural miracle when he seared Sodom and Gomorrah off his planet. No natural explanation would do.

23 How could Moses have spent forty years in the desolate badlands on the border between what is now Israel and Egypt, with 2 to 3 million refugees? That's a bit like Chicago in Death Valley.

What to believe. Math or miracles?

Here's the back story.

When the stubborn Egyptian king finally released the Jews from slavery, Moses got them the dickens out of Dodge.

They headed into the barren Sinai Peninsula, a badlands that would serve quite nicely as a penal colony or a retirement home for select politicians, all telephone solicitors, and a few distant relatives who aren't distant enough.

Here's the Bible math: "There were about six hundred thousand men on foot, plus all the women and children" (Exodus 12:37).

To be exact: "The grand total of men who were at least 20 years old and eligible for military duty was 603,550" (Numbers 1:45–46).

Let's say that on average there was one woman for every man and two kids for every couple—in a day when couples often had many more kids than that.

Total: about 2.5 million souls.

That's roughly the population of Chicago, the third most populated city in the United States, after New York City and Los Angeles.

Let's say they crossed through the path God made for them in the sea and that they walked nearly shoulder to shoulder in lines about 100 yards wide. The back line would have been about 20 miles behind the front line.

After the crossing, the Bible says these refugees spent forty years in the barren Sinai badlands—a Mars-like deathtrap with little water and not much green to sink their teeth into.

Under these conditions, some Christians wonder if the Bible got its math right. Bible experts have been working the numbers and coming up with ideas.

It is what it is

Many Christians say the numbers are not symbolic. The tally represents an actual census.

Plenty of Bible experts say they take this approach. Yet when asked how two million hungry, thirsty souls could survive in the bone-dry badlands south of Israel for forty years, many simply say they have no idea how God pulled it off. (See question 48: "To feed Moses and the Jewish refugees, God sent enough white-flake manna and fresh quail to feed them all. We're supposed to swallow that?")

"It seems best for us to remain agnostic on this matter," wrote Peter Enns, a biblical studies professor writing in the *NIV Application Commentary.*

Wrong census

Some scholars say the census wasn't of the Jewish refugees. It was a census of the Jewish nation at the time the story was put down in writing. They say that was sometime after the Jews settled in what is now Israel—perhaps during the time of King David.

Others argue: That's not what the Bible says.

Wrong word

The Hebrew word for "thousands" is *elep*. It can also mean "families" or "clans," which were extended families, such as one family, including the grown children and their families.

If the Bible writer intended to report on about 600 clans, the number of Jewish refugees may have been closer to 20,000. That's still a lot of people trying to survive in the badlands.

If the Bible writer intended to report 600 individual families— let's say four per family—Moses may have led as few as 2,500 refugees.

Coded message in the number

Like many ancient languages, Hebrew letters pulled double duty. They not only spelled words, they represented numbers. Think A=1, B=2.

When you tally the numbers of the letters for "sons of Israel," a popular way of describing the Jews, you get the number 603,551.

That's just one soul higher than reported in the census given to Moses. If you add Moses, it's a perfect match.

As this theory goes, the Bible writer was trying to say that Moses led out of Egypt all the "sons of Israel," however many there were.

24 How could killing a goat get rid of a person's sin?

Sin is a capital offense as far as God is concerned, Bible writers say. God made that clear enough in the beginning when he gave the first couple just one rule to obey: "You must never eat from the tree of the knowledge of good and evil because when you eat from it, you will certainly die" (Genesis 2:17).

It's as though sin and holiness can't be in the same vicinity. That might explain why God gave Adam and Eve the divine boot out of Eden after they sinned.

Abel, son of Adam and Eve, was the first on record in the Bible to sacrifice an animal to God: "Abel also brought some choice parts of the firstborn animals from his flock. The Lord approved of Abel and his offering," (Genesis 4:4).

People throughout the ancient Middle East sacrificed animals to their gods. It was a familiar ritual long before Moses came along and declared it God's official law for the Jews.

As the Bible puts it, God told Moses to explain the sacrificial system this way: "The life of each creature is in its blood. So I have given you the blood of animals to pay for your sin on the altar. Blood is life. That is why blood pays for your sin" (Leviticus 17:11 NIRV).

Humans sin. They deserve to die for it, Bible writers teach. But God allows guilty humans to pay for their sins by killing animals as substitutes.

PETA would not approve.

Why does God need blood? Wouldn't a sincere apology do?

An apology is pretty much what one of the Bible songs said God wanted anyhow: "Offerings and sacrifices are not what you want. The way to please you is to feel sorrow deep in our hearts. This is the kind of sacrifice you won't refuse" (Psalm 51:16–17 CEV).

Bible experts are left to speculate about why God chose the sacrificial system as the way for Jews to repent of their sins.

A few guesses:

- **Sacrifices were common.** This was already a well-known worship custom. God simply adapted it for the Jewish people.
- **Sacrifices showed how deadly serious sin is.** The rituals of an animal sacrifice engaged all the senses with graphic reminders of one critical lesson: the price of sin is death.

- *Sight*: cutting the animal's throat
- *Sound*: the animal's death squeal
- *Touch*: butchering the warm animal
- *Smell*: aroma of barbecued meat
- *Taste*: worshipers ate some sacrifices

Jews had sacrificed animals to God for several centuries before Moses.

Abraham, the father of the Jews, is famous for almost sacrificing his son. But God gave Abraham a last-second substitute: "When Abraham looked around, he saw a ram behind him caught by its horns in a bush. So Abraham took the ram and sacrificed it as a burnt offering in place of his son" (Genesis 22:13).

Jews continued offering sacrifices for some 2,000 years—until the Romans leveled the Jerusalem temple while crushing a Jewish revolt in AD 70.

That temple was the one and only place Jews were allowed to offer sacrifices, and it has never been rebuilt.

Jews no longer sacrifice animals. Instead, they ask God's forgiveness through prayer.

But as the Bible tells it, Jews have been doing that all along, in addition to offering sacrifices: "Let my prayer be accepted as sweet-smelling incense in your presence. Let the lifting up of my hands in prayer be accepted as an evening sacrifice" (Psalm 141:2).

New Testament writers describe Jesus as the sacrifice to end all sacrifices: "He offered a sacrifice once for all, when he gave himself" (Hebrews 7:27 CEV).

25 When bachelor Paul told women to be quiet in church and always do what their husbands say, was he really speaking for God—and to women throughout all time?

Hear the word of the Lord, from Paul.

Let your women keep silent in the churches, for they are not permitted to speak. . . . And if they want to learn something, let them ask their own husbands at home; for it is shameful for women to speak in church. . . . The things which I write to you are the commandments of the Lord.

1 Corinthians 14:34–35, 37 NKJV

Let a woman learn in silence with all submission. And I do not permit a woman to teach or to have authority over a man, but to be in silence.

1 Timothy 2:11–12 NKJV

These words that Paul wrote in two letters are why many churches refuse to ordain women ministers—churches like the Southern Baptists, America's largest Protestant church group.

Christians who say Paul was talking about all women in all churches for all time generally insist that men and women are equal in God's sight, but that they have different roles to fill in the church: Men do the talking in public, and women hold down the home front and help at church in supporting roles. But women don't preach. And they don't teach men in Sunday school classes.

Scholars call this the complementary view because men and women complement each other by fulfilling their God-given tasks to get the job done.

Some women today don't seem to feel the compliment.

Lots of Christians argue that Paul wasn't laying down a new law for all time. They say he was tackling problems in those two particular churches: one church in what is now Corinth, Greece, and another church in Ephesus, on the west coast of Turkey. What problems the women may have been causing is anyone's guess.

One popular thought is that in Corinth, the women were going overboard with their newfound gift of speaking in tongues during worship services. Speaking in tongues is an ecstatic, heavenly language that sounds like gibberish to most listeners, but that is supposed to have an interpretation, which God provides through another person in the group.

A clue that connects women to this problem: the language Paul used to address the matter.

When Paul urged speakers in tongues not to disrupt the worship service if they didn't have an interpreter, he said: "Let them be silent in church" (1 Corinthians 14:28 NRSV).

A few sentences later, he added, "Women should be silent in the churches" (1 Corinthians 14:34 NRSV).

Paul used the same Greek verb in both sentences: *sigao*. It means "Keep silent." Or not so politely, "Shut up."

Another reason many Christians say Paul couldn't have intended for all women in all churches for all time to be quiet is that he complimented some women leaders who didn't seem constrained by the complementary view.

These women prayed and prophesied in church meetings, as Peter reported, quoting an ancient prophecy he said had been fulfilled: "I will pour out my Spirit even on my servants—men and women alike—and they will prophesy" (Acts 2:18 NLT).

Junia, one woman Paul commended, may have been an apostle— a top leader of the Christian movement: "Greetings to Andronicus and Junia, my relatives, who were in prison with me. They are very important apostles" (Romans 16:7 NCV). Some Bible translations, however, suggest the couple was considered important *by* the apostles, not *as* apostles.

Even though many churches today say they welcome the idea of women ministers, few hire them. A male minister leads nine out of every ten churches in the United States.

26 Why do Christians say hell is a fiery place of eternal torture? Bible scholars say *hell* is just an English word invented to translate *Hinnom* (Hebrew) or *Gehenna* (Greek), the name of a valley on Jerusalem's south side.

Hinnom became more than a valley to the Jews. Much like September 11, 2001, became more than a day on the calendar to Americans.

Hinnom Valley, like September 11, came to represent a fiery terror.

Many Jews believed they lost their country because of what happened in that valley. It was there that two of their kings—Ahaz and his grandson, Manasseh—actually sacrificed their sons to idols: "He [Ahaz] offered sacrifices in the valley of Ben-Hinnom, even sacrificing his own sons in the fire" (2 Chronicles 28:3 NLT).

Some Jews saw this as the worst of Israel's many sins, and one of the reasons God unleashed judgment day in 586 BC. Babylonian invaders from what is now Iraq decimated the Jewish homeland, leveled Jerusalem, and deported many survivors.

After that, Jews linked the name of Hinnom Valley to judgment day.

In fact, all twelve times the valley is mentioned in the New Testament—usually by Jesus—it's a metaphor describing a place of fiery punishment.

Jesus: "If your hand causes you to sin, cut it off. It's better to enter eternal life with only one hand than to go into the unquenchable fires of hell [*Gehenna*] with two hands" (Mark 9:43 NLT).

Bible translators try to capture that idea of a place of fiery punishment—*Gehenna*—by using the English word *hell* instead of the name of the valley.

27 Why would a loving God condemn anyone—even humanity's worst offenders—to never-ending torment in fire?

Jesus paints a terrifying picture of hell.

• **Barbecue.** "Everyone will be salted with fire" (Mark 9:49).
• **Torture.** "He went to hell, where he was constantly tortured. . . . He yelled, 'Father Abraham! Have mercy on me. . . . I am suffering in this fire'" (Luke 16:23–24). That's from a parable.
• **Forever.** "The fire is never put out" (Mark 9:48).

Christians struggle over what to make of hell.

Some take the Bible descriptions literally.

Others say they can't imagine the likes of Jesus Christ lighting the eternal flame—forever barbecuing the people he died to save.

Besides, they ask, "What's the redemptive value of torturing someone forever?" Whenever God punished anyone in the Bible, it was to direct them or others out of harm's way. Hell keeps them in harm's way forever.

Other Christians argue that the redemptive value of hell is that it proves the justice of God and glorifies his holiness.

Here are a few theories Christians have suggested about hell.

Hotspot

It's a place of eternal fire and torment. Descriptions in the Bible aren't just metaphors. They're real: "Those whose names were not found in the Book of Life were thrown into the fiery lake" (Revelation 20:15). Listen for a splash and a yowl, because the burning lake is as real as lava. And it's going to leave a mark.

Rationale: God isn't just loving. He's holy. And he's just. That means he doesn't hang out with evil. And he doesn't ignore evil. He gives evil what it deserves.

God-free zone

There's no torturous fire in this spiritual realm. But there's no God, either. People who wanted nothing to do with God in life get their wish in the afterlife. That's the torment—being forever separated from God.

Rationale: We shouldn't read the descriptions literally because though hell is often described as fire, it's also described as darkness: "Throw this useless servant outside into the darkness. People will cry and be in extreme pain there" (Matthew 25:30).

Dead end

The fire symbolizes annihilation. Sinners won't suffer forever, but their destruction will last forever.

Rationale: "Don't be afraid of those who kill the body but cannot kill the soul. Instead, fear the one who can destroy both body and soul in hell" (Matthew 10:28).

Do-over

We get a second chance. Confronted with Jesus in the afterlife, nonbelievers will admit they were wrong about him.

Rationale: (1) "At the name of Jesus everyone in heaven, on earth, and in the world below will kneel and confess that Jesus Christ is Lord" (Philippians 2:10–11). (2) "All the broken and dislocated pieces of the universe—people and things, animals and atoms—get properly fixed and fit together in vibrant harmonies, all because of his death, his blood that poured down from the Cross" (Colossians 1:20 THE MESSAGE).

28 Shouldn't we be a tad skeptical when we read that Abraham and Sarah had their first son, Isaac, when he was 100 and she was 90?

Seventy-year-old Rajo Devi Lohan, of India, might have believed it. That's how old she was when she gave birth to a daughter in 2008. She's the oldest woman on record in modern times to give birth to a baby. There are other women who were reportedly older—as old as seventy-three—but their ages can't be confirmed.

Yet the story of Abraham and Sarah kicks old-age pregnancy up a notch or two. The Bible writer says that even Abraham and Sarah couldn't believe it when God told them they would have a baby.

Sarah: "She laughed to herself. She thought, 'I'm worn out, and my husband is old. Can I really know the joy of having a baby?'" (Genesis 18:12 NIRV).

Abraham: "He laughed as he thought to himself, 'Can a son be born to a hundred-year-old man? Can Sarah, a ninety-year-old woman, have a child?'" (Genesis 17:17).

Some say God showed his sense of humor when he named the child "Laugh." That's pretty much what *Isaac* means. Scholars translate it with a variety of kissing cousin words:

- *laughter*
- *he laughed*
- *to laugh*

Perhaps God named the boy Isaac to remind Sarah and Abraham how they reacted to him. More likely, scholars say, it's a description of their joy in finally having a child of their own.

Maybe, too, it's an inside joke: God getting the last laugh along with the pleasure of seeing how happy Sarah and Abraham were with their boy.

Who knows?

As for who's going to believe that this couple had a child at such ripe old ages, most Christians either embrace the Bible story as accurate or they postpone judgment on details such as the math.

Perhaps, some speculate, the writer exaggerated the ages of the father and mother of the Jewish people as a way to honor their memory. A bit like a director might do when a film is "based on a true story."

As the Bible tells it, "Sarah lived to be 127 years old" (Genesis 23:1) and "Abraham lived 175 years" (Genesis 25:7).

29 If God knows everything, why did he test Abraham's faith by asking him to sacrifice his own son?

L ord, even before I say a word, you already know it" (Psalm 139:4 NCV).

But was God so clueless about Abraham that he had to give him a pass/fail test?

That's not what most Bible experts say was going on in this odd story. They say the test wasn't a tool for teacher God to evaluate student Abraham, to see if Abraham's faith measured up. It was more like a talent show than a test. Put a gifted person on stage and then watch him wow the world—and himself.

Abraham had already shown remarkable faith by moving, at God's command, from a cultured civilization into the boonies of what is now Israel. Beyond that, Abraham consistently obeyed God—doing everything God asked. Including circumcising himself, which any guy with a sharp knife would agree is asking a lot.

Because of Abraham's faith, God gave him a son: Isaac. God promised to make Abraham's family into a great nation of people, through this son. All of Abraham's hopes rested on this boy, "your only son Isaac, whom you love" (Genesis 22:2).

Perhaps God wanted Abraham and the world to see that all of Abraham's hopes, in fact, rested on God.

It's just a guess. The Bible writer doesn't explain why God ordered Abraham to sacrifice his only son, and then aborted the sacrifice at the last second.

But the theory seems to track with something Jesus said: "Well-meaning family members can be your worst enemies. If you prefer father or mother over me, you don't deserve me. If you prefer son or daughter over me, you don't deserve me" (Matthew 10:36–37 THE MESSAGE).

God comes first.

Some would say it's only fair, since God put us first. He did for us what Abraham was willing to do for God: sacrifice his son.

Many Bible experts say they see in Abraham's story a foreshadowing of what God would do for humanity some 2,000 years later when he sent Jesus to die on the same ridge of hills where many say Abraham nearly killed Isaac: Moriah, known today as Jerusalem.

30 Why do rich people think they're going to heaven, given what Jesus and James said about the rich?

It is easier for a camel to go through the eye of a needle than for a rich person to enter the kingdom of God.

Jesus, Mark 10:25

Your greedy luxuries are a cancer in your gut, destroying your life from within. You thought you were piling up wealth. What you've piled up is judgment.

James 5:3 THE MESSAGE

Rich women bankrolled Jesus and his disciples. So it seems like a fair guess that Jesus thought as kindly of them as they did of him. The sugar mommas were Mary Magdalene, who would be among the first to see the resurrected Jesus, along with Susanna and Joanna—whose husband was King Herod's administrator.

These and other women "provided financial support for Jesus and his disciples" (Luke 8:3).

Not all rich people are selfish, exploitive, and spiritually bankrupt. Only some. Perhaps most, if the Bible's apparent prejudice against the rich is any clue.

There's a heaping helping of Bible verses that trash the rich for the low-blow methods many of them use to get rich and stay rich:

- write laws to favor themselves
- buy off politicians and judges—and in our day hire top lawyers while the poor are assigned assistant public defenders
- underpay workers
- cheat customers
- ignore the poor

Rich people tend to treasure their treasure more than they treasure God's treasure. They build *their* kingdom instead of God's kingdom.

We can't become citizens of God's kingdom when we're obsessed with our own. That's the point Jesus was trying to make, most scholars agree.

Jesus used an exaggerated illustration to drive home his point: an image of the largest critter in the region trying to squeeze through the smallest hole people could imagine—a camel through the eye of a needle.

Jesus loved hyperbole: "Why do you see the piece of sawdust in another believer's eye and not notice the wooden beam in your own eye?" (Matthew 7:3).

The warning that Jesus and James were both making is summed up nicely in this one-liner from Jesus: "Your heart will be where your treasure is" (Luke 12:34).

The man who donated his tomb for the burial of Jesus is a wonderful example of a rich guy experiencing a change of heart. Joseph of Arimathea was a wealthy member of the top Jewish council—the supreme court that orchestrated Jesus' execution. Joseph was also a closet follower of Jesus. He came out of the closet at the crucifixion, asking Roman governor Pilate for the body of Jesus.

"Joseph took the body and wrapped it in a clean linen cloth. Then he laid it in his own new tomb" (Matthew 27:59–60).

Joseph apparently respected Jesus more than he coveted the respect of his colleagues. He put Jesus first, and he likely paid the price for it with diminished returns in his kingdom on earth. He may well have lost his seat on the council, suffered the cold shoulder of his Jewish business associates, and watched the value of his assets take a dive into the dirt.

Certainly he would have been concerned about this. But he seemed more concerned about God's kingdom than his own—as though his heart had found something new to treasure.

31 Why did Jesus seem to paint God as a genie waiting in heaven to grant our every wish: "Have faith that you have already received whatever you pray for, and it will be yours"?

Bible experts take this quote from Jesus (Mark 11:24) in different directions, but not generally in the direction of Aladdin's lamp. Or a wishing well.

Prayer didn't work out that way for Jesus.

On the night of his arrest, a few hours before his morning crucifixion, he prayed, "Father! You can do anything. Take this cup of suffering away from me" (Mark 14:36). God the Father did nothing of the kind.

Paul didn't always get what he prayed for either: "I was given a problem that caused pain in my body. . . . Three times I begged the Lord to take it away from me. But he said to me, 'My grace is all you need'" (2 Corinthians 12:7–9 NIRV).

Some scholars link Jesus' perplexing words to a story Mark had just reported. Jesus had chased off salespeople who were hawking their wares at the Jerusalem temple. Jesus then dissed the temple leaders who had allowed the practice and may have taken a cut from the sales: "Scripture says, 'My house will be called a house of prayer for all nations,' but you have turned it into a gathering place for thieves" (Mark 11:17).

On the neighboring hillside, a ridge called the Mount of Olives, Jesus pointed to "a mountain"—scholars often guess it was the hilltop crowned by the massive temple. With everyone looking at that hill, Jesus said anyone with faith "can say to this mountain, 'Be uprooted and thrown into the sea,' and it will be done for him" (Mark 11:23).

Many scholars read between the lines, and add a little history. The temple mountain did, in a way, get tossed into the sea. Romans destroyed the temple in AD 70, and the Jews never rebuilt it. If the scholars are right, Jesus was saying that prayer isn't tied to the temple even though the temple was supposed to be "a house of prayer."

Instead, prayer is based on faith. Not just any faith. Certainly not faith in the magical power of words spoken in a sacred space, such as the temple. Effective prayer is based on faith in our relationship with God. It's that close relationship that keeps us from asking for stuff that doesn't really matter much in God's kingdom.

And it's that close relationship that produced responses like these.

- *Jesus, after asking God to spare him from the crucifixion:* "But let your will be done rather than mine" (Mark 14:36).
- *Paul, stuck with a mysterious problem that God wouldn't take away:* "Now I take limitations in stride, and with good cheer. . . . I just let Christ take over! And so the weaker I get, the stronger I become" (2 Corinthians 12:10 THE MESSAGE).

32 Some well-respected archaeologists say Jericho was a ghost town by the time Joshua got there. What evidence is there to support the Bible story?

Okay, that's two questions in one.

The first is implied: Why do some archaeologists say Jericho was a ghost town when Joshua arrived?

The second is clear enough: What's the counterpoint?

Question 1: Why no evidence of an invasion?

Most archaeologists—not necessarily Christians—say there's no evidence of life in Jericho at the time of Joshua. Nor any evidence of an attack on the city—or of a conquest of what is now Israel.

Many students of the Bible, however, warn that it's a bit risky to say something didn't happen just because we haven't found the evidence yet.

A few years ago, many Bible scholars said King David was probably just a folklore legend—like King Arthur and his Knights of the Round Table. They argued that if he had ever lived, there would be archaeological evidence about him.

As it turns out, there is. But it didn't start surfacing until 1993. That's when his name first showed up engraved in ancient Hebrew on a stone tablet found in Israel. The engraving dates to about a century after his lifetime. That was just the first of several ancient references to David that have been discovered recently.

Just as scholars once doubted David's existence, many Bible experts and historians say Joshua and the Jews probably never invaded Israel—because there's no evidence to support the Bible's story about massive battles and crumbling cities.

90

Some scholars offer alternative theories.

The most popular: Jewish herders nibbled their way into Israel. In other words, it wasn't a military campaign that got them there. It was greener grass.

Jewish families, one at a time, migrated into Israel in what became a gradual and peaceful relocation. Only centuries later did they unite, overpower the locals, and set up Israel as a Jewish nation.

Question 2: Was Jericho really a ghost town?

Yes, most archaeologists agree—with a minority opinion that begs to differ.

Based on excavations by Kathleen Kenyon from 1952 to 1958, the majority opinion is that Jericho—a speed bump of a city, about the size of ten football fields—fell at least 150 years before Joshua got there.

Kenyon said Jericho died in about 1550 BC, though Bible experts say Joshua didn't show up there until about 1400 BC, or perhaps in the 1200s BC; that's another hot debate—the timing of the Exodus.

Kenyon based her date mainly on pottery she found there. And on pottery she didn't find: imported Cyprus pottery, common from 1550 BC–1400 BC. Pottery came in different shapes, sizes, and designs—like cars do today. That made it easy to date the layers of the ruin in which the pottery was found. If you find a Ford Mustang in a mound of dirt that used to be Dodge City, you can pretty well guess that you're not poking around in Wyatt Earp's barn.

Other archaeologists—the minority opinion—say they disagree with Kenyon's findings. John Garstang, digging in Jericho during the 1930s, said Jericho fell in the 1400s BC. More recently, archaeologist Bryant Wood said he agreed with Garstang, adding that Kenyon misidentified the local pottery styles, which he said do include some pottery from the 1400s. In addition, he said Kenyon shouldn't have expected to find imported Cyprus pottery in the section of Jericho where she dug—the poor side of town.

91

One shred of evidence that supports the Bible story: jars full of springtime grain. Typically, invaders looted the town, taking everything they could carry—especially food for the road. But for Joshua's Jews, everything in Jericho was off limits—as an offering "claimed by the Lord" (Joshua 6:18).

Many Christians insist that it's too early to write off the Bible's invasion story as fiction. Just because archaeologists haven't yet found compelling evidence of cities wiped out by Jewish invaders in Joshua's time doesn't mean they never will. And even if the evidence never turns up, many archaeologists admit, there's a limit to what archaeology can tell us about the past.

With that in mind, many Christians choose to give the Bible writer the benefit of the doubt.

 33 Why did Joshua order a man and his entire family stoned to death and burned only because the man took a few valuables from Jericho—a city the Jews had just destroyed, killing everyone? The man's family hadn't done anything.

It sounds a bit like a racial joke: A Jew walks into a city full of dead people. He walks out with a nice robe, a sack of silver, and a bar of gold. What happens next?

Nothing good.

The Jewish militia gets defeated in its next battle—thirty-six Jews killed in action. Stunned at losing what should have been a given, Joshua tore his clothes and then tore into God: "Almighty Lord, why did you bring these people across the Jordan River?

Was it to hand us over to the Amorites so that they could destroy us?" (Joshua 7:7).

God told Joshua that someone had disobeyed his order.

Once the city of Jericho fell, everything in it was off limits—devoted as an offering to God. The Hebrew word for this ban is *herem*, related to the Arabic word *harem*—which refers to a man's gallery of wives.

The women in the harem were off limits to all men but the husband. The contents of Jericho were off limits to everyone but God.

As the Bible writer reports the story, God told Joshua what to do with the guilty man: "The man who is selected, along with everything he has, must be burned because he has stolen what the Lord has claimed" (Joshua 7:15).

A man named Achan admitted the crime. Joshua took him, his family, his livestock, and all of his possessions into a valley. There, the Jews stoned them all and then burned the bodies.

There are at least three ways to take this story.

1. **God ordered the mass execution**, in which case Bible experts have some explaining to do.
2. **God ordered only the guilty man's execution**; Joshua added the family and livestock for good measure.
3. **God had nothing to do with the execution**; an editor who compiled the stories presumed God ordered the executions because that's what happened, and God controls everything that happens.

It doesn't take much explaining for approaches two or three. They either make sense to us or they don't.

But the idea that God ordered the slaughter of Achan's entire family doesn't make sense at all. Not to most people. Even the law of God prohibited executing innocent people: "Each person must be put to death for his own crime" (Deuteronomy 24:16).

Bible experts offer suggestions for understanding why Achan and all he owned had to die.

Ripple effect. Just as one person, such as Abraham or Jesus, can bless many people with wonderful gifts, one person can curse many people with tragic consequences. A rotten king can lead a nation to disaster. And a lousy father can do the same to his family and his community.

Holiness in the sinner's house. Achan's secret treasures weren't just battlefield mementos. They were sacred, holy items that belonged to God. Achan brought holiness into his sinful tent. Sin can't survive that. Even Moses could not have handled getting close enough to God to see his face: "No one may see me and live" (Exodus 33:20). Everything sinful that came into contact with God's holiness had to be destroyed.

For many devoted Christians, explanations like these don't ring true.

These Christians say they believe the story as it's told, but they still don't understand why everyone in Achan's family had to die. Yet what they lack in understanding, they seem to make up for in faith. They say we must trust the justice of God, though in this instance it's hard to see it.

34 Daniel's prophecies about the Greek empire track nicely with what happened. Isn't that a clue that someone wrote it after the fact—as history instead of prophecy?

M any Bible experts insist that Daniel wrote the Bible book named after him. The fact that he got so many of his predictions right—400 years ahead of time—is nothing more than proof that he was the genuine article, an honest-to-goodness prophet.

Many others say someone wrote them in Daniel's name, perhaps to remind the Jews that God had a long history of taking care of his chosen people. At the time the "predictions" were written, according to this theory, an invader from what is now Syria was trying to wipe out the Jewish religion: Antiochus IV Epiphanes (215–164 BC).

So it wasn't as though the writer was fibbing. He was telling history in a way to help his fellow Jews see God at work in the past and to encourage them to believe that God would be with them in the days ahead, too.

Here are some of the predictions that scholars say track perfectly with history.

Warrior king

"A warrior-king will come. He will rule a vast empire and do as he pleases. But as soon as he is established, his kingdom will be broken into pieces and divided" (Daniel 11:3–4).

Alexander the Great ruled the Greek Empire 336–323 BC. He died shortly after conquering the Middle East. His generals divided his empire.

Peace treaty sealed by marriage

"After a few years the southern and northern kings will make an alliance. The southern king's daughter will go to the northern king to make peace" (Daniel 11:6).

The two biggest pieces left over from Alexander's mega Greek Empire were Ptolemy in the south (Egypt) and Seleucid in the north (Syria, Iraq, and Iran). The northern king (Antiochus II Theos, who ruled 261–246 BC) exiled his wife, Laodice, so he could marry Berenice, daughter of the southern king (Ptolemy II Philadelphus, who ruled 285–246 BC).

The ex makes a comeback

"She [the southern king's daughter] won't hold on to her power, and the alliance won't last" (Daniel 11:6).

Laodice managed to get back home and snuggle up with the king who had dumped her.

It was all an act; she wanted revenge. She poisoned the king, orchestrated Berenice's assassination, and declared her son the new king.

An eye for an eye

"The southern king will be outraged. He will go to fight the northern king, who will raise a large army that will fall into the southern king's hands" (Daniel 11:11).

The southland had a new king. He was Berenice's brother, Ptolemy III Euergetes (who ruled 246–221 BC). His army invaded the northland empire, pushing as far as Babylon, near modern Baghdad, Iraq.

Daniel's incredibly accurate links to history continue until about 164 BC. After that, some scholars say, his predictions seem to go wrong. The guess is that this is when the person writing in Daniel's name must have lived. Not being a prophet, this writer got the future wrong.

Reading the prophecy as prophecy

Other Bible scholars say Daniel's predictions simply haven't been fulfilled yet, or they relate to another time in history.

For example, one popular question from Daniel's prophecies spins around trying to identify a ruler who desecrates the Jewish temple in Jerusalem: "At the place of worship, a desecrating obscenity will be set up and remain until finally the desecrator himself is decisively destroyed" (Daniel 9:27 THE MESSAGE).

Some who read most of Daniel's prophecies as history written during Greek times speculate that the bad guy was King Antiochus IV Epiphanes, who converted the temple of God into a temple for Zeus.

But folks who read this prophecy as a prediction suggest the evil ruler might have been General Titus of the Roman Empire. His men destroyed the Jerusalem temple in AD 70. The temple has never been rebuilt. That's because Jerusalem's most famous landmark has been resting there for 1,300 years: a Muslim shrine, the Dome of the Rock.

Other folks who read Daniel's prophecy as prophecy say his mystery man might be an evil ruler yet to come—perhaps the evil beast that John described in the last book of the Bible:

> This second Beast worked magical signs, dazzling people by making fire come down from Heaven. It used the magic. . . . to animate the image of the Beast so that it talked, and then arrange that anyone not worshiping the Beast would be killed.
>
> Revelation 13:14–15 The Message

35 Was God okay with polygamy? Some of God's favorite people—such as Jacob, David, and Solomon—had a harem of wives.

True enough, the Jewish law seems to presume some Jewish men will have more than one wife: "A man might have two wives and love one but not the other" (Deuteronomy 21:15). That's the first line in a Jewish law that urges men to treat the children of both wives fairly.

The man who delivered this law to the Jews—Moses—had two wives: Zipporah and an unidentifed woman from Cush, a land somewhere in what is now Egypt or Ethiopia.

Abraham, father of the Jews, had a wife, Sarah, and a concubine, Hagar, who had been Sarah's servant. A concubine was a second-class-citizen sort of a wife. In Abraham's case, Hagar functioned as a surrogate mother, providing Abraham with a son after it seemed that Sarah would never get pregnant.

Jacob, father of the men whose families would produce the twelve tribes of Israel, had four wives. And, it seems, four times the trouble of a man with one wife.

Most Bible experts say we shouldn't read these stories and jump to the conclusion that God was okay with polygamy. Writers were simply reporting the facts.

Laws that dealt with polygamy were attempts to deal with realistic situations in that culture—not attempts to encourage the behavior that the laws were trying to protect people from.

God's ideal marriage situation, most Bible experts agree, shows up in the creation story. One man. One woman.

Jewish law started the process of steering men away from marrying a bevy of beauties. In a day when people measured the worth of a king by the size of his harem, Jewish law warned: "The king must never have a large number of wives" (Deuteronomy 17:17).

In most Bible stories about men with many wives—Abraham, Jacob, David, Solomon—the tale of their family life reads like the script of a reality TV show that everyone would want to watch, but no one would want to live.

One of David's sons raped a half-sister. The full brother of the victim pulled off a hit on the rapist and later attempted a coup against his dad.

Solomon's thousand wives led the wise old man into a world of stupidity: "Solomon built an illegal worship site on the hill east of Jerusalem. . . . He did these things for each of his foreign wives who burned incense and sacrificed to their gods" (1 Kings 11:7–8).

Not a happy ending.

There's one other possible clue about what God thinks about marriage. It comes in a quote from Jesus, who was talking about life after death: "When the dead come back to life, they don't marry. Rather, they are like the angels in heaven" (Mark 12:25).

That's a swing of the pendulum—from polygamy to celibacy.

But others might say that's comparing apples to oranges: souls limited with physical bodies to souls enjoying their perfected bodies with capabilities we can't begin to imagine.

36 The only rule God gave Adam and Eve was to not eat fruit from the tree of knowledge about good and evil. What does God have against people knowing the difference between right and wrong?

When God created Adam and Eve and planted them in the Garden of Eden, he gave them just one rule, as the Genesis writer tells it: "You are free to eat from any tree in the garden. But you must never eat from the tree of the knowledge of good and evil because when you eat from it, you will certainly die" (Genesis 2:16–17).

Sadly, the writer skipped the details that any thinking person would want—and could get by asking the most basic follow-up questions.

- What exactly was the fruit from the tree of knowledge? It could have been an apple since they grow in the Middle East.

But given the variety of fruit there, and the odds against an apple, we wouldn't want to bet on that in Vegas.

• What made the fruit a killer? Was it toxic?
• What's wrong with knowledge? Does God want a monopoly on it?

Here are a few educated guesses from Bible educators, the top scholars.

It was a test

If humans were to live in freedom, some scholars say, they needed to be free to make their own choices—to obey or disobey God.

So God gave them a choice.

It was a test. Would the first humans be loyal to God? Or would they do as they pleased, regardless of what God said?

They did as they pleased. And in the process, they proved two things: (1) humans are free to make their own decisions; (2) they have to take responsibility for their decisions.

The fruit wasn't poisonous

God's death sentence, as it's phrased in the original Hebrew language, reads much like the warnings in later prophecies: "That wicked person will die because of his sin" (Ezekiel 33:8).

The implication in the Genesis lingo isn't that the fruit itself would kill Adam and Eve, but that humanity's first couple would suffer the consequences of breaking God's law. They would be sentenced to death.

Theories about the tree of knowledge

God wasn't prohibiting Adam and Eve from getting smarter, most Bible experts agree. Something else was going on. Among the many guesses, here are two:

Tree of consequences. "Knowledge of good and evil" doesn't describe what kind of insight a person gets from eating the fruit. It describes the consequences of obeying or disobeying God. If Adam and Eve had obeyed God by not eating the fruit, they would have known good. But because they ate the forbidden fruit, they knew evil.

Tree of wisdom without respect for God. "Knowledge of good and evil" simply describes wisdom, a wonderful aspiration—but only when it's teamed with respect for God: "Search for wisdom as if it were money and hunt for it as if it were hidden treasure, then you will understand the fear of the Lord" (Proverbs 2:4–5).

Adam and Eve chased wisdom, but in the process, they ran away from God. Their sin was in choosing to become self-dependent instead of dependent on God. The consequences: they got their wish. As a result, they had to live with those consequences—all the way to the grave.

37 The Bible says "sons of God" had sex with human women, who gave birth to giants. Doesn't that sound a little like Greek mythology?

Yep, many Bible-believing Christians would agree—the story sounds like a myth.

The gents in the story may not have been angels, many Bible experts argue. Yet most Jewish and Christian scholars in ancient times said they were. And many scholars today agree.

Here's the story:

> The sons of God noticed that the daughters of men were beautiful. They looked them over and picked out wives for themselves. . . . Giants came from the union of the sons of God and the daughters of men. These were the mighty men of ancient lore, the famous ones.
>
> Genesis 6:2, 4 THE MESSAGE

Who were the "sons of God"? There are two main theories today.

An angel of a husband

Ancient Jewish writers said the sons of God were angels.

That's how Jewish scholars translated the phrase into Greek when they created the first known Bible translation more than a century before Jesus. Instead of "sons of God," they used the phrase *angels of God.*

A Jewish book written about the same time the translation was going on—1 Enoch—tells a tale that sounds a lot like the Genesis story:

- Two hundred "angels, the children of heaven" lusted after the beautiful daughters of men.
- The angels descended to Mount Hermon, in what is now northern Israel.
- They married human women.
- The women gave birth to giants, each giant stretching almost a mile (1.6 km) high. That's taller than three Empire State Buildings.

Jesus seemed to throw a wrench into the working gears of that theory. He said angels don't do that sort of thing: "When the dead rise, they won't get married. . . . They will be like the angels in heaven" (Mark 12:25 NIRV).

What about the angels down here? Would angels on earth like to party? That might be a follow-up question some would want to ask Jesus.

A prince of a husband

"Sons of God" doesn't always refer to angels.

Sometimes "sons of God" refers to humans, especially top dogs such as kings, nobles, and other alpha males.

- **Description of Israel's judges:** "You are gods. You are all sons of the Most High" (Psalm 82:6).
- **God speaking of King Solomon:** "I will be his Father, and he will be my Son" (2 Samuel 7:14).

As for their children being giants—called *Nephilim*—many Bible scholars say it's not clear whether the children are:

1. giants
2. normal but heroic children from the marriage of "sons of God" and human women.

The Genesis writer mentions the *Nephilim*, a term some Bibles translate as "giants" (Genesis 6:4 THE MESSAGE) or "heroes and famous warriors" (NLT).

Nephilim is a mysterious word used just one other time in the Bible. There it describes tall men whom Joshua and other Jewish scouts saw in the Promised Land: "We saw Nephilim there. . . . We felt as small as grasshoppers, and that's how we must have looked to them" (Numbers 13:33).

But the Genesis writer doesn't describe them as giants or as children from the marriage between sons of God and human women. Bible scholars have to presume that from the context. And many scholars insist it's a fair and logical presumption. Even so, most admit that the facts aren't clear in the original language.

38 Would a loving God really put a good man like Job through horrible suffering just to test his loyalty?

As the story goes, God allowed a mysterious person identified simply as "the Accuser"—not necessarily the devil—to test the righteousness of Job through suffering.

Job lost all of his children in a windstorm. He lost all of his herds to raiders and natural disasters. And finally, he lost his health.

Not all Bible experts read Job's story as history. Some read it as fiction, a story intended to make a spiritual point—a bit like the parables of Jesus.

The point in Job's story: Don't presume that people who are suffering are being punished by God for something they did.

The counterpoint was a common belief in Bible times: God made some folks rich to bless them for being good and he sent misery to other folks to punish them.

Jesus' disciples seemed to believe it, too. When they saw a man born blind they asked Jesus, "Why was this man born blind? Was it because of his own sins or his parents' sins?" (John 9:2 NLT).

One reason some scholars guess that Job's story is fictional is the extensive dialogue. A couple of obvious questions:

Who was taking notes?

What human being could possibly take notes that detailed without a recording device or remarkable skill in shorthand?

Yet many Christians—probably most—insist Job was a real human being whose story has been preserved through the inspiration that God's Spirit provided to the anonymous writer. And based on clues in the story, they speculate that Job lived about the time of Abraham, father of the Jews. That's back in the days when some people in the Middle East still wrote in cuneiform, pressing wedge-shaped marks into soft clay. A slow process for anyone taking notes during a debate.

These Christians defend God, arguing that he wasn't the mastermind behind the evil directed at Job. The Accuser is the one responsible for all the rotten things that happened to Job.

This Accuser, whom some Christians link to the devil, is responsible because he sent the tragedies into Job's life. And he did it for an unholy reason: to discredit God by proving him a liar. God had said Job was a righteous man. The Accuser said Job was merely a man on the take from his Divine Sugar Daddy—righteous only as long as the sugar kept coming.

God and Job in a tag team effort proved the Accuser wrong.

In the process, they also delivered an important message to human beings everywhere: don't presume that people who are suffering deserve to suffer.

If there's a moral to the story, it might go something like this: It's better to be kind to a suffering soul than to throw salt on their sores as Job's "friends" did—Zophar told Job, "You haven't gotten half of what you deserve" (Job 11:6 THE MESSAGE).

39 Psalm 44:23 says, "Wake up, O Lord! Why do you sleep? Get up!" (NLT). Does God catch Zzz's?

It might come as a surprise, but some scholars argue that people in Bible times believed God slept.

After all, the Bible says when God finished his six days of creation, "he rested on the seventh day" (Genesis 2:1 KJV). And there are other psalms that talk about God sleeping: "Wake up, my God" (Psalm 7:6); "Wake up, and help me" (Psalm 59:4).

Jews also heard stories popular throughout the ancient Middle East about other gods sleeping, so it was a common idea at the time. And in those myths they heard, sleeping often represented power. A god could afford the luxury of sleep because nothing threatened him. He had no equal.

Jews might have figured that described their one, true God, the Lord of all.

Most Bible scholars, however, say God doesn't need to catch Zzz's.

For one thing, there are Bible passages that say so:

"The Guardian of Israel never rests or sleeps. The Lord is your guardian" (Psalm 121:4–5).

For another, the psalms are song lyrics. Poems.

Poets don't think like normal people. They don't write like normal writers. They don't always say what we think they mean.

Psalm 44 is the blues—a lament.

The poet was upset because his people, presumably the Jews, had gotten overrun by invaders.

"Wake up!" isn't a poet trying to shake God to his senses and roll him out of bed. It's a cry for help.

The song is also a search for answers. The poet doesn't understand why God let this happen to his people: "We had been true to the covenant you made with us. . . . Why do you turn your face away from us? . . . Rise up and help us. Save us because of your faithful love" (Psalm 44:17, 24, 26 NIRV).

The book of Psalms is a collection of songs that cover a wide range of raw human emotions. There are lots of happy songs thanking God for his kindness. But there are plenty of complaints, lots of anger and grief, along with pleas for forgiveness. If it's an emotion we can feel, it probably shows up in a song of Psalms.

40 "We know that all things work together for the good of those who love God—those whom he has called according to his plan." How would you explain that idea to a Holocaust survivor? Or to just about anyone at a funeral?

Not all Christians read Romans 8:28 as God's promise to everyone everywhere for all time.

Some don't even read it as God's promise to anyone.

They read it as one line of a letter from a preacher to a church. Period.

The apostle Paul wrote these words to Christians of a fledgling church in Rome. Perhaps, some Christians speculate, this promise was merely one preacher's attempt to encourage some new Christians who were suffering persecution from Jews—Christians who might soon face lions in the arena, once Roman leaders joined the mob.

Most Christians, however, say they believe that Paul was speaking for God.

Those are the Christians who have some explaining to do. On two fronts:

A promise limited

The first point they make, generally, is that this promise isn't for everyone. Paul limits the promise to "those who love God." But that really doesn't seem to help much, as far as many folks are concerned.

The fact is, life's fertilizer hits the fan and blows all over Christians, too. Christians suffer tragedies like anyone else. What's good about that?

Redefining *good*

It's impossible to climb inside Paul's head and read his brain like a book, to find out what he was thinking.

Theologians and preachers try. It's in their job description.

Here are a few of the more popular guesses about what Paul had in mind.

Good means making us more like Christ. Hardship changes us. Think of the hardship as a sculpture's chisel. We lose part of ourselves in the sculpting. And it hurts. But in the end, we'll look more like Jesus.

This interpretation comes from the verse Paul wrote immediately after the promise: "God planned that those he had chosen would become like his Son" (Romans 8:29 NIRV).

Good means salvation. It's not just that we become more like Jesus, other Christians argue. We become saved. That's the big point Paul was making in this part of his letter, some scholars say.

"God planned for them to be like his Son; and those he planned to be like his Son . . . he also made right with him" (Romans 8:30 NCV).

Good means embracing God's love. Some scholars say that's what's good about the stuff of life—whether the stuff is a stroke or a poke. In the end it lifts us up and places us into the arms of a loving God.

I'm absolutely convinced that nothing—nothing living or dead, angelic or demonic, today or tomorrow, high or low, thinkable or unthinkable—absolutely *nothing* can get between us and God's love because of the way that Jesus our Master has embraced us.

Romans 8:38–39 THE MESSAGE

41 The Bible says, "Prayer offered in faith will heal the sick." If that's true, why aren't doctors out of business?

If James 5:15 was ever true—that prayer is a cure-all for sickness—it's sure not true today.

Some Christians come down hard on sick folks, accusing them of not having enough faith to get well. Big mistake, according to most scholars.

It's not the sick person who needs the faith. It's the person *praying* for the sick person: "prayer offered in faith."

So, if we ever find ourselves sick when a well-meaning Christian friend comes along and says we need more faith, we should probably ask our friend to pray for us. Then when we don't get well, we can tell our friend it's his fault for not having more faith.

What was James thinking? That's the question scholars ask about this passage in the Bible.

Healing miracles were going on during the early years of the Christian movement. Some scholars say those healings were God's way of helping jump-start Christianity by convincing nonbelievers to believe. That would explain why healing miracles diminished over time.

But even during the early years, prayer didn't always cure sick people.

Paul had some mysterious affliction: "a thorn in my flesh" (2 Corinthians 12:7 NLT). He prayed for a cure that never came. Instead of curing him, the Lord told him, "My grace is enough for you. When you are weak, my power is made perfect in you" (2 Corinthians 12:9 NCV).

Prayer with caveats

It's not the spoken words of prayer that can—at least sometimes—heal the sick, most Bible experts say.

It's prayer *with caveats* that work wonders—caveats that give God the final say: "Have them pray for you and anoint you with olive oil in the name of the Lord" (James 5:14).

"**Anoint you with olive oil.**" This wasn't a magic trick in the Bible. It was a ritual that religious people, such as Jewish priests and church leaders, did to dedicate people to God—to place them in God's service and to entrust them to God's care. Anointed souls in Old Testament times included children, kings, and prophets. And at least by New Testament times, the sick were added.

"**In the name of the Lord.**" When we say this phrase, we're not only invoking the power of Jesus, we're asking that our request line up with God's plan. So say many students of the Bible.

Paul reflected this deferential attitude toward God when he found out he would never get over his affliction—whatever it was. He said he figured the Lord would somehow make good use of this weakness. And he moved on with his life.

Jesus showed the same attitude when he asked God to cancel the crucifixion, but added: "However, your will must be done, not mine" (Luke 22:42).

Physical healing or spiritual?

One other theory is that James wasn't talking about physical healing at all. He was talking about the spiritual healing that comes through confessing our sins and receiving God's forgiveness.

James did say that sick people should confess their sins: "So admit your sins to each other, and pray for each other so that you will be healed" (James 5:16).

But most Bible experts say James was talking about people who were physically sick, and that this reference to sin and forgiveness is a kind of P.S. to the paragraph.

If most Bible experts have it right, we should pray for sick people, believing that God can heal them, but trusting God to do what is best.

42 Jonah's prophecy that Nineveh would fall in forty days didn't come true. Why doesn't that make him a fraud?

Moses put it this way: "If a prophet speaks in the Lord's name and what he says doesn't happen or come true, then it didn't come from the Lord" (Deuteronomy 18:22).

Try tossing that line out to reel in Jonah. See if he bites.

He made the long walk from what is now Israel to a city in what is now northern Iraq: Nineveh. On orders from God, he delivered this message: "In forty days Nineveh will be destroyed" (Jonah 3:4).

Simple enough. This capital of the Assyrian Empire is toast.
Didn't happen.

The king of Nineveh, horrified at Jonah's prophecy, immediately led his citizens into a time of mourning and repentance.

His hope: "God may reconsider his plans" (Jonah 3:9).

God did. He spared the city.

Most Bible experts say it's not that God changed his mind. It's that the people changed. So God adapted his plans to the new situation.

Jonah, however, was bummed that his prediction didn't come true: "Just kill me now, Lord! I'd rather be dead than alive if what I predicted will not happen" (Jonah 4:3 NLT).

What Jonah didn't seem to realize, most scholars say, is that he was one of the few prophets in the Bible who succeeded in doing what prophets are supposed to do: Turn people away from sin and toward God.

So did Moses get it wrong? Jeremiah, too? He said, "A prophet who predicts peace must show he is right. Only when his predictions come true can we know that he is really from the Lord" (Jeremiah 28:9 NLT).

Moses and Jeremiah weren't wrong, scholars insist. They were simply speaking to their immediate situations. They weren't offering a rule for all time.

Even Jeremiah, in a different situation, acknowledged that God can change his plans after a prophet predicts doom: "I may threaten to tear up, break down, and destroy a nation or a kingdom. But suppose the nation that I threatened turns away from doing wrong. Then I will change my plans" (Jeremiah 18:7–8).

With that in mind, most Bible experts don't label Jonah a fraud. They call him a rare success.

43 God ordered Joshua and the invading Jews to kill everyone who lived in what is now Israel—men, women, children, and even the animals. Why would God do such a thing?

Kill all the people and animals" (Deuteronomy 20:16 CEV). "Anything that breathes" (NRSV).

That's what Moses said God wanted the Exodus Jews to do once they invaded what is now Israel: Kill all the men, women, and children. Even the livestock.

Bible writers rarely answer the "why" questions behind God's laws. This law is a rare exception.

Why genocide?

Moses' answer: "If you don't destroy them, they'll teach you to follow all of the things the Lord hates. He hates the way they worship their gods. If you do those things, you will sin against the Lord your God" (Deuteronomy 20:18 NIRV).

Bible scholars say that some of the local worship rituals included child sacrifice and sex with temple priests and priestesses.

Here are a few facts of history, as preserved in the Bible. The Jews

- didn't annihilate the locals
- did learn to live alongside them as neighbors
- did pick up their religion, as Moses had warned

Moses predicted all of this, according to the Bible. He also seemed to predict what God would do about the Jews slipping into idolatry. Speaking of the future, but in the past tense—as though it had already happened—Moses said:

You worshiped worthless idols, and made me jealous and angry! Now I will send a cruel and worthless nation to make you jealous and angry. . . . I wanted to scatter you. . . . But I dreaded the sound of your enemies saying, "We defeated Israel with no help from the Lord."

Deuteronomy 32:21, 26–27 CEV

Some scholars say this entire chapter—written as a poem—was probably crafted about the time of the other major prophets—about a thousand years after Moses. Three reasons:

1. It's written in the past tense.
2. It accurately describes Jewish history.
3. The style of writing tracks with that of classical Jewish prophecies, many of which were written as poems.

The history this seems to have been describing:

Assyrians from what is now Iraq wiped the northern Jewish nation of Israel off the map in 722 BC, deporting the survivors. Babylonians of Iraq did the same to the southern Jewish nation of Judah in 586 BC.

At that point, there was no Jewish nation.

Some fifty years later, Persians from what is now Iran defeated the Babylonians and freed the Jews to go home and rebuild their capital city of Jerusalem.

Christians read the genocide command of Moses in different ways.

God gave the order. Moses gave the command to wipe out the locals, but that command came from God. God doesn't have to justify his justice. The annihilation seems harsh to us. But God was working with a group of homeless refugees in an attempt to build a nation of people devoted to him—not to fake gods.

God didn't give the order. Moses may have dreamed up the order. Or perhaps it came from an editor piecing together the story hundreds of years later. Maybe he took a look at the facts of history and then made presumptions about God's role in the story—figuring that if the Jews slaughtered the Canaanites, God must have ordered it, since God is the director of world history, especially everything Jewish.

44 Why does the Bible praise a man who sacrificed his own daughter?

Here's the dumb vow Jephthah, a Jewish general, made to God. He said if God let his army win the upcoming battle, "then whatever comes out of the doors of my house to meet me when I return safely from Ammon will belong to the Lord. I will sacrifice it as a burnt offering" (Judges 11:31).

Was he drunk when he made this incredibly stupid vow? What did he expect to come out and greet him when he came home from war? A goat?

His only daughter came running to him—dancing and playing a tambourine. "Oh no, Daughter!" Jephthah said, "What disaster you've brought me! I made a foolish promise to the Lord. Now I can't break it" (Judges 11:35).

Jephthah gave his daughter two months to prepare, and then he "did to her what he had vowed" (Judges 11:39).

Burnt offerings got their throats cut. The worshiper then cut the body into pieces and burned it all on a stone altar that would have looked a bit like a campfire.

Bible scholars do not defend Jephthah. He didn't have to kill his daughter. He had other options.

Ignore the vow. Jewish law made it illegal to sacrifice humans: "They [non-Jews] commit every imaginable abomination with their gods. God hates it all with a passion. Why, they even set their children on fire as offerings to their gods!" (Deuteronomy 12:31 THE MESSAGE).

Pay the fee. If Jephthah had known Jewish law better, he would have known about this option: "The Lord spoke to Moses, 'Tell the Israelites: If any of you makes a special vow to give a person to the Lord, you may give money instead of the person'" (Leviticus 27:1–2).

The fee was four ounces (113 grams) of silver for a girl. That's about the weight of a roll of twenty quarters. Value: $80 when silver sells for $20 an ounce.

Take the punishment like a man. If Jephthah figured God would punish him if he broke the vow—though the Bible gives no indication God would do any such thing—Jephthah could have decided to take whatever came. He could have taken the hit instead of forcing his daughter to take it.

Another head-shaker is why the writer of Hebrews included Jephthah in a list of Jewish heroes who "conquered kingdoms, did what God approved, and received what God had promised" (Hebrews 11:32).

Perhaps it's because in spite of his ignorance, Jephthah did show that he respected God. Jephthah actually did what Abraham, father of the Jews, was prepared to do: sacrifice his child. In Abraham's case, an angel stopped him at the last moment: "Do not lay a hand on the boy" (Genesis 22:12).

45 People in the early church were "baptized for the dead." Isn't that a bit late?

The best guess about the meaning of this passage (1 Corinthians 15:29 NIV), as far as many Bible scholars are concerned, is that *Christians were getting baptized for other Christians who died before they got a chance to get baptized.*

Maybe the dead Christian converted during a terminal illness, or got run over by a donkey cart on the way to the river.

In any case, the baptism could have been a bit like a parent picking up a dead child's high school graduation certificate. It publically honors the deceased, while at the same time celebrating the person's accomplishments, values, and dreams.

This reference to folks getting baptized on behalf of the dead is an odd sound bite mentioned only once in the Bible—and without any explanation. It was only a passing comment in a letter Paul wrote to Christians in Corinth, Greece.

That's the trouble with reading someone else's mail. We get in on only part of the conversation.

Here's what was going on in that section of the letter:

Paul was defending the resurrection. Some folks in the Corinth church didn't seem to believe in it. So Paul gave them a series of if/then arguments to help make his case.

If the dead aren't raised, then:

- Jesus wasn't raised (1 Corinthians 15:13).
- My preaching is worthless (v. 14).
- Your faith is worthless (v. 14).
- There's no reason to get baptized for the dead (v. 29).
- Christians are the most pitiful people on the planet (v. 19).

Since Paul's letter is the only reference to people getting baptized for the dead, some scholars speculate that it wasn't a widely practiced ritual.

A few scholars have floated the idea that Christians were getting baptized for non-Christians. But most Bible experts say that doesn't track with the teachings of Paul or Jesus. Both taught that we're saved through our faith in Jesus, not by someone else's ritual on our behalf after our corpse is lying dead in the dirt.

46 Speaking of his return, Jesus said, "This generation will not disappear until all these things take place." That was fifty generations ago. Why do Christians still talk so much about the second coming of Jesus?

Some Christians obsess over the second coming because:

• They're naturally curious.
• A good many writers know they can make money by feeding that curiosity with imagination passed off as news—fiction as fact.

At least that's what more than a few Bible experts would say.

In fairness, most end-time writers insist that they believe what they write about the signs of an imminent second coming. But plenty of Christians question their interpretations of the Bible as well as their motives for writing.

What Jesus had to say about the second coming is convoluted and hard to unravel. Most Bible experts admit that.

Some scholars say Jesus made a bad call about the second coming—that he missed his prediction about coming back during that generation.

Others say he did no such thing. They say he wasn't predicting the second coming within a generation, but that he was predicting the destruction of the Jerusalem temple—which did happen within a generation. Romans leveled it in AD 70, about forty years after Jesus. That temple has never been rebuilt.

Jesus' speech in Matthew 24—along with similar versions in Mark 13 and Luke 21—starts with his pointing to the huge temple complex that dominated Jerusalem and saying, "You see all these buildings, don't you? I can guarantee this truth: Not one of these stones will be left on top of another. Each one will be torn down" (Matthew 24:2).

Much of what follows in his speech tracks nicely with the history that leads up to the Jewish revolt against Rome in AD 66 followed by Rome's merciless response: crushing the revolt and leveling Jerusalem.

- **"Many . . . will say, 'I am the Messiah'"** (v. 4). Jewish historian Josephus (37 BC–AD 101) confirmed there were many who made that claim.
- **"Wars and rumors of wars"** (v. 6). Jews talked about a revolt for many decades beforehand.
- **"Famines and earthquakes"** (v. 7). Jewish historian Josephus wrote of famines during the first century. The Bible tells of an earthquake when Jesus died: "The earth shook, and the rocks were split open" (Matthew 27:51).
- **"Those of you in Judea should flee to the mountains"** (v. 16). Many Christians in the Jerusalem area seemed to remember Jesus saying this, because when they got word of the Romans coming, they fled. Church historian Eusebius, writing in the AD 300s, said they left because of "a revelation."
- **"Disgusting thing . . . in the holy place"** (v. 15). Roman soldiers desecrated the temple, destroying it.

What's confusing about Jesus' speech is that he seemed to talk about more than just the end of the temple. He also seemed to weave in references to his second coming.

The big question is this: Was he talking about both when he said, "This generation will not disappear until all these things take place" (Matthew 24:34)?

Some say he was, and they creatively redefine "this generation" as "this human race." Most scholars say that's a stretch, of taffy proportions.

Many others say Jesus was referring only to the temple. They say that when Jesus spoke about the timing of the second coming, he said, "No one knows when that day or hour will come. Even the angels in heaven and the Son don't know. Only the Father knows" (Matthew 24:36).

47 Why does the Bible say homosexuality is a sin? Don't science and our own observation suggest that some people are naturally homosexual?

Christians are at each other's throats over this question—at least in some churches—debating what to do about homosexuality. Many churches forbid homosexuals from joining their community of faith. Other churches ordain them as ministers. That's how far apart Christians are on this controversial topic.

Most churches pitch their tents in one of three major camps:

- **I'm okay, you're okay.** Homosexuality is as natural as heterosexuality.
- **Gay is okay if you don't have sex.** There's nothing wrong with having homosexual desires, but it's a sin to act on those desires by engaging in homosexual sex.
- **There's nothing okay about gay.** Homosexuality—the orientation as well as the act—is a sin requiring forgiveness and, if possible, healing.

There's nothing okay about gay

Christians in this camp take their cue from the Bible, which in all the main English translations certainly seems to condemn homosexuality.

- "It is disgusting for a man to have sex with another man" (Leviticus 18:22 CEV).
- "When a man has sexual intercourse with another man as with a woman, both men are doing something disgusting and must be put to death" (Leviticus 20:13).
- "No one who is immoral . . . is unfaithful in marriage or is a pervert or behaves like a homosexual will share in God's kingdom" (1 Corinthians 6:9–10 CEV).
- "We also know that the law is not made for good people. . . . It is for people who are against God and are sinful . . . who take part in sexual sins, who have sexual relations with people of the same sex" (1 Timothy 1:9–10 NCV).

Christians who have pitched their theological tents in this camp say that if we take the Bible seriously and treat it as the Word of God, there's no way we can do what is politically correct: accept homosexuality.

Instead, we have to do what is biblically correct: reject homosexuality as sinful. If we don't, we find ourselves among an unfortunate group of souls: "How terrible it will be for people who call good things bad . . . who think darkness is light . . . who think sour is sweet" (Isaiah 5:20 NCV).

The spiritual cure for homosexuality, as far as these Christians are concerned, is the same as it is for any other sin: repentance and forgiveness.

Beyond that, some Christians say, homosexuals may be able to experience physical healing, as well. Through counseling, prayer, and the work of the Holy Spirit, a homosexual can become a

121

heterosexual. There are Christians who identify themselves as heterosexuals healed of their former homosexual desires.

Many Christians in this camp acknowledge that not all homosexuals will be freed of their attraction to the same sex. Counselors advise homosexuals who convert to Christianity to treat their desire the same way the apostle Paul treated his mysterious "thorn in the flesh," a difficulty he never identified: "I was given a problem that caused pain in my body. . . . Three times I begged the Lord to take it away from me. But he said to me, 'My grace is all you need. My power is strongest when you are weak'" (2 Corinthians 12:7–9 NIRV).

Gay is okay if you don't have sex

Christians in this camp have a lot in common with Christians who say "There's nothing okay about gay."

Both groups treat the Bible as God's Word—something that should not be ignored or overruled by conventional wisdom or political correctness.

The biggest difference is that Christians in this group see absolutely nothing wrong with having homosexual desires. They would compare that desire to any other sinful desire or temptation we might experience. There's nothing wrong with the desire or the temptation. It's wrong only when we give in to that sinful desire.

Many Christians in this group seem willing to accept the idea that some people may be naturally oriented toward homosexuality. Some compare this to the way many folks seem wired with a predisposition toward addictive behavior—folks who become alcoholics and drug addicts.

Alcoholics Anonymous teaches that if you're an alcoholic, you're an alcoholic for life. Your lifelong task is to stay away from alcohol.

In much the same way, a homosexual may be homosexual for life.

Some Bible-revering, tradition-minded Christian counselors are beginning to acknowledge that attempts to straighten out a gay person generally don't work. Dr. Mark A. Yarhouse, professor of psychology at Regent University—founded by Pat Robertson, chairman of the conservative Christian Broadcasting Network and a former Southern Baptist minister—put it this way in his book *Homosexuality and the Christian*:

> A realistic expectation would not be a categorical change (from completely gay to completely straight), but rather modest shifts along a continuum of attraction.

I'm okay, you're okay

Some Christians say there is absolutely nothing wrong with homosexuality—in orientation or in sexual activity.

The question for many other Christians is this: How do pro-gay Christians justify their end run around what the Bible says on the topic?

Here comes a scholarly term: Wesleyan Quadrilateral.

Scholars who have studied the life and teachings of John Wesley (1703–1791), founder of the Methodist church, have come to the conclusion that when he faced tough theological problems, he studied them from four angles:

Bible—What does the Bible say about it?

Tradition—How have Christians throughout the centuries dealt with it?

Reason—What seems like a reasonable way to deal with it?

Experience—What does our personal experience suggest we do about it?

As far as many Christians in this camp are concerned, the Wesleyan Quadrilateral vote comes out in a dead heat—two votes against accepting the homosexual lifestyle to two in favor.

Two votes against: *The Bible* says "don't." *Tradition* is obvious; the church has a long history of rejecting homosexuals.

Two votes for: *Reason* says it makes sense for us not to tell someone else whom they can and can't love. *Experience* reminds us that even among our own circle of family and friends, some are wired with same-sex desires.

Reason and experience seem to get a boost from science:

American Academy of Pediatrics: "Counseling may be helpful for young people who are uncertain about their sexual orientation. . . . Therapy directed specifically at changing sexual orientation is contraindicated, since it can provoke guilt and anxiety while having little or no potential for achieving changes in orientation."

American Psychiatric Association: "The APA opposes any psychiatric treatment, such as 'reparative' or 'conversion' therapy, which is based upon the assumption that homosexuality per se is a mental disorder or based upon the . . . assumption that a patient should change his/her homosexual orientation."

But what about the Bible? It's God talking, many Christians insist. And he says "don't."

A tiny minority of Christians say the Bible translators got it wrong.

For example, the *Queen James Bible*, a gay-friendly translation, says one writer was talking about heterosexual men who were having sex with male prostitutes in pagan temples: "Thou shalt not lie with mankind as with womankind in the temple of Molech: it is an abomination" (Leviticus 18:22).

The presumption: normal gay sex is okay.

Most Bible experts would call that creative and wishful thinking.

It's more common for Christians in this camp to approach the Bible's anti-gay passages this way:

Jewish law is obsolete. "Faith in Christ has come. So we are no longer under the control of the law" (Galatians 3:25 NIRV).

Paul was quoting the obsolete law. When Paul wrote in his letters that homosexuality is sinful, he was drawing from his studies as a Pharisee, an expert in Jewish law—remarkably, the same laws he said elsewhere were obsolete. That leaves some folks trying to figure out which Paul to believe—Paul who rejected the law or Paul who rejected homosexuality because the law forbids it.

When in doubt, follow Jesus. Jesus never talked about homosexuality. But he did talk about judging others and loving others.

Most Christians who embrace homosexuals as full members within the community of faith put more theological weight on those teachings. They argue that the rule of love trumps the obsolete Jewish law about homosexuality as well as the anti-gay teachings of Paul, a former Pharisee who they say may have been deferring to Jewish law.

Love others. "Let me give you a new command: Love one another. In the same way I loved you, you love one another. This is how everyone will recognize that you are my disciples—when they see the love you have for each other" (John 13:34–35 THE MESSAGE).

Don't judge. "Don't judge others, or you will be judged. . . . You hypocrite! First, take the wood out of your own eye. Then you will see clearly to take the dust out of your friend's eye" (Matthew 7:1, 5 NCV).

Gay minister V. Jill Sizemore, senior pastor of Metropolitan Community Church in Knoxville, Tennessee, told me that when she has to deal with "those stubbornly ensconced in their argument of the infallible word of God," she appeals to love: "Put down the book that you would use to hurt me. Look into my eyes and tell me that you would have me scorned, bullied, discriminated against. . . . Now who is the pervert?" She said that in her view, "Love trumps all arguments that clearly favor injustice of any kind."

Many Christians, however, insist that God isn't just about love. He's about holiness, too. And they say their Bible teaches that homosexuality is sin—and that God won't stand for it.

Several Christian denominations have split over the question of what to do about gay believers.

125

48 To feed Moses and the Jewish refugees, God sent enough white-flake manna and fresh quail to feed them all. We're supposed to swallow that?

The manna story is tough for many people to sink their teeth into because there's no natural explanation for it. We can't figure out where it came from.

The quail story, on the other hand, has some compelling evidence from Mother Nature.

As the Bible writers tell it, Moses and the Jewish refugees of the Exodus out of Egypt were into their second month in the Sinai badlands.

They were hungry and complaining that they were going to starve.

God told Moses, "I'm going to send you food from heaven like rain. Each day the people should go out and gather only what they need for that day" (Exodus 16:4). Jews called the food *manna*, Hebrew for "What is it?"

"The manna was like coriander seeds. It looked like sap from a tree" (Numbers 11:7 NIRV).

"It was white and tasted like wafers made with honey" (Exodus 16:31).

Jews gathered the flakes, crushed them into flour, and baked them into patties of sweet bread.

One attempt at a natural explanation: It was bug poop from sapsuckers.

Aphid-like insects called manna mealybugs (*Trabutina mannipara*) suck sap from the Sinai tamarisk tree (*Tamarixgallica*).

They excrete sweet balls that dry into pale-colored flakes forming a crust on branches and plant stems. Sinai herders call the flakes manna, and use it as a sweetener.

There are two problems with that explanation, in addition to it being bug poop.

First, there aren't enough mealybugs to feed thousands of people. A few herders, though.

Second, mealybugs produce their sweet balls only in May and June. But the Jews ate manna year-round, "for 40 years until they came to a place to settle" (Exodus 16:35).

It's possible, some scholars say, that a writer or an editor exaggerated the story. A few flakes became a heaping helping and forty days became forty years.

Most Christians, however, don't discount the possibility that God used some other resource we haven't yet discovered—or he performed a creation-style miracle, whipping up a nice mess of "What is it?" for his people.

Quarter-pounders to go

As the Bible tells it, the Jews got tired of manna. They wanted meat.

If the most popular guess about what God sent them is right, they got their fill of quarter-pounders.

"The Lord sent a wind from the sea that brought quails and dropped them all around the camp. . . . The people went out and gathered the quails" (Numbers 11:31–32).

There are ancient paintings that show Egyptians picking up quail like they're picking squash from a garden. Apparently, the birds on a layover were too tired to move.

A natural explanation of what happened is that an exhausted migrating flock of stubby quail (*Coturnix coturnix*) landed near the camp.

These quail still migrate each spring from Africa to Europe. They weigh in at about a quarter pound (113 g) and stretch half the length of a foot-long dog (15 cm).

49 Why does the New Testament describe Samson as a hero of the faith? Almost everything he did seems driven by revenge or lust.

Samson wasn't just his own snowflake—unique in many ways. He was a flake—a selfish jerk.

It's tough to say anything good about him once we've read his tale. Nearly everything he did seems selfish.

Samson's story, as reported in the Bible, has little to do with his strength. Instead, his entire story spins around his weakness for women and the trouble it got him into.

He married a Philistine. Samson married a Philistine woman, over his parents' strong objection: "Aren't there any women among our relatives or all our people? Do you have to marry a woman from those godless Philistines?" (Judges 14:3).

He declared a private war on the Philistines. At the wedding, Samson made a bet with his Philistine guests that they couldn't solve his riddle. But they bullied Samson's bride into charming the secret away and reporting it to them. Samson lost the bet and had to pay up with one set of clothes for each of the thirty men.

He stormed off to a neighboring Philistine city, killed thirty Philistines, and took their clothes back to pay off the debt. Then he went home to Mom and Dad—without his bride. By the time he cooled off and went back to get his wife, her dad had married her off to the best man.

That set off a chain of tragic, retaliatory events: Samson vs. Philistines.

- **Samson: Operation Foxfire.** Samson caught 300 foxes, tied torches to their tails, and set them loose to burn Philistine grain fields, vineyards, and orchards.

- **Philistines: Operation Blazing Lady.** Philistines responded by burning to death Samson's ex, along with her dad.
- **Samson: Operation Butcher Block.** Samson "attacked them violently and slaughtered them" (Judges 15:8).
- **Philistines: Operation Catch the Hairball.** Philistines sent their army into Jewish territory to kill or capture Samson by terrorizing his people, the Jews.
- **Samson: Operation Fake Out.** When Samson's fellow Jews pleaded with him to stop the Philistine pillaging by turning himself in, he agreed. It's the single unselfish scene in his story. After his capture, he broke free and killed 1,000 of the Philistines who had arrested him.

Samson's date with a prostitute. Everyone needs a little down time. Samson decided to relax with a Philistine prostitute in Gaza.

Some men in the city decided to attack him when he came out, weakened from sex.

He came out so energized at midnight that he ripped the city gate off its hinges and carried it forty miles (64 km) before he set it on a hilltop near the Jewish city of Hebron.

Samson met his fatal attraction. Samson fell in lust—or maybe love—with another Philistine woman, Delilah.

She was so *not* a good girlfriend.

When Philistine leaders heard about Samson's new gal, they bribed Delilah into helping them capture Samson. She nagged out of him the secret of his strength: long hair. Then she arranged for a haircut. A little off the top.

She did it while he napped with his head on her lap.

When Samson woke, the Philistines arrested him, popped out his eyeballs, and used him like a mule—powering a grist mill to grind grain into flour.

Samson's suicide. The Philistines paraded him into their temple during a festival to honor their god. It was a kind of victory dance to show that their god, Dagon, was stronger than Samson's God.

By then, Samson's hair had grown back. He prayed his only reported prayer. Even it sounds selfish. Standing between two pillars that supported the temple, he prayed, "God, give me strength just one more time! Let me get even with the Philistines for at least one of my two eyes" (Judges 16:28).

He pushed on the pillars, which may have been made from blocks of rock or wood mounted on top of each other. The temple collapsed, and Samson died with the Philistines who had crowded into the building.

It's unclear why one anonymous writer in the New Testament included Samson on a list of Jewish heroes of the faith along with Gideon, David, and Samuel—men who "ruled with justice, and received what God had promised them" (Hebrews 11:33 NLT).

Perhaps it's because when push came to shove—as it often did with Samson—he trusted God as the source of his strength for the battles he felt compelled to fight and the pillars he needed to dislodge.

Some historians say that Samson's legacy assured Israel's survival. Before he came along, the kingless Jews were in the process of becoming assimilated into the culture of their stronger neighbor; the Philistines had learned the secret of forging iron.

Samson forever changed the relationship by driving a wedge of distrust and anger between the two nations.

In time, the Jews would emerge as winners in the war for the Promised Land. King David managed to outmuscle the Spartan-like Philistines.

50 God's prescribed diet for the Jews included crickets, locusts, and grasshoppers, but no lobster, shrimp, or soft-shell crab. What does that say about God's opinion of Jews?

Where's a Jew going to find seafood in the Sinai badlands? That's where the Bible says they were when Moses gave them their kosher food laws.

The Sinai does, however, host crickets, locusts, and grasshoppers—protein.

Not as tasty as buttered lobster, but the creepy crawlers were actually something the Jews could put in their mouths and chew. Lobster would have been a pretend meal.

Beyond that, the Jewish menu makes no sense. Not from a dietary point of view. Most Bible experts admit that.

Some Bible students speculate that God scratched pork from the menu because it had to be cooked longer to kill dangerous parasites such as Trichinella. Or maybe he dropped it because pigs ate more food than they were worth—which explains why we call some hearty eaters "pigs" or "porkers."

But even if that's why God decided Jews shouldn't lean on pork, there are still lots of questions about why he nixed other healthy treats.

Rabbit and camel—both forbidden—are just as nutritious as goat or lamb, which are kosher. And rabbits are free, if you can beat them to the hop.

One popular guess about the reason for the limited menu: *It wasn't the meat that mattered. It was the obedience.*

God was creating a nation from a motley crew of refugees. He wanted to train them to obey, much like parents train their children.

So God gave the Jews rules to follow. These rules weren't just a test of obedience. They became an exercise regimen—a tool for building their spiritual muscle. If they could manage to obey God in small matters, such as a menu, they'd be better energized to obey in big deals—like attacking walled cities to recapture the land God promised to their ancestor Abraham.

Kosher food laws also helped distinguish the Jews as a nation devoted to God.

We can tell the Amish by their clothes, their buggies, and their really good pies. They're pretty handy with wood, too. People in Bible times, as today, could tell observant Jews by the food they ate, the gods they refused to worship, and the way they spent their Saturdays: resting and worshiping God.

But when it comes right down to it, and we ask Jews why they eat only kosher food, many will simply say it's because the Torah tells them to. *Torah* is what they call the first five books of the Bible, which contain the Jewish laws: Genesis, Exodus, Leviticus, Numbers, and Deuteronomy.

51 What was fair and righteous about Noah putting a curse on his grandson, Canaan, for something the boy's father did?

There's nothing fair about it.

Nor is there anything particularly righteous about Noah getting drunk and naked—which is what started the fiasco.

Noah's youngest son, Ham, saw him lying in his tent—under-dressed for just about any occasion but skinny-dipping or streaking across a college campus in the 1970s.

Ham could have shown some respect and covered his dad. Instead, he had show-and-tell. "He went outside and told his two brothers" (Genesis 9:22).

The older brothers averted their eyes from their dad as they backed into the tent and covered him.

When Noah sobered up and found out what Ham had done, Noah put a curse on Ham's youngest son: "Canaan is cursed! He will be the lowest slave to his brothers" (Genesis 9:25).

No one knows why Grandpa Noah skipped a generation and put a curse on his grandson Canaan, who had apparently done nothing wrong, but who had the misfortune of being born into Ham's family.

Theories about why Noah targeted Canaan:

- **Grumpy old man.** It was a typical family feud. Noah was lashing out at his son. He figured the best way to hurt him was to hurt his son.
- **Planning ahead.** The story symbolizes Israel's future dominance over the descendants of Canaan, which include the Canaanites and the Egyptians. Some Jews considered Noah's curse fulfilled when Joshua and the Exodus Jews invaded and eventually conquered the Canaanite homeland, now called Israel.

Not all stories in the Bible are examples of godly people doing godly things. Some Bible stories are the kind of ditties we write about in our private journals and hope no one ever reads.

Noah may have felt that way about this one.

52 God says it's a sin for Jews to charge interest to each other, but they can charge interest to anyone else. Why the discrimination?

It's true. The Bible says that one of the hundreds of laws God gave Moses to pass on to the Jews was this one: "Never charge another Israelite any interest on money, food, or anything else that is borrowed. You may charge a foreigner interest, but not an Israelite" (Deuteronomy 23:19–20).

The Bible says this in several sections in the Jewish books of law, including Exodus 22:25 and Leviticus 25:36.

Sadly, the Bible writers never answer the why question: Why could Jews charge interest to non-Jews, but not to Jews?

When scholars start looking for clues to this mystery, some like to start with the Hebrew word for "interest." It's not an upbeat word. But it's a word we can sink our teeth into. Literally, it's "bite." As in a loan officer telling a customer: "Sure, I'll take a bite out of you."

That's not something we should say to our family or friends. And that's one of several guesses as to why Moses gave his people this law. The Jews were a family.

Don't profit off your family. When Moses delivered these laws, the Jews were a ragtag assortment of related refugees who had just fled Egypt. They were an extended family. They needed to build themselves into a nation. Moses didn't want them to swap resources within their ranks. He wanted them to grow their resources by drawing from other people who could afford it.

Don't exploit the poor. If a Jew couldn't profit off a fellow Jew in a loan deal, why would any Jewish businessman bother loaning to a fellow Jew? Even if the fellow Jew was starving for a loan. Why bother? There's no money in it.

Jewish law seemed to anticipate that motivation problem. That would explain why it forbids Jews from ignoring the poor— including poor people of other races and religions:

> If any of your people become poor and unable to support themselves, you must help them, just as you are supposed to help foreigners who live among you. Don't take advantage of them by charging any kind of interest or selling them food for profit.
>
> Leviticus 25:35–36 CEV

Don't deprive a hurting farmer or herder. Bible historians say that most loans in this agricultural society were intended to help farmers and herders through hard times: crop failure or a livestock-killing drought. The law forbidding interest on a loan made it easier for struggling farmers and herders to get their businesses back up and running.

The loophole

As Jewish commerce expanded beyond farming and herding during the Middle Ages, it got harder for Jews to follow their Jewish law about charging interest. Loans with interest became necessary. People needed capital to start up a city bakery, a carpentry shop, or to hire seasonal help. Jews with money to invest wanted some return on their investment in these non-emergency situations.

The Jews created what seemed like a loophole. It was a legal device they called "permission of business." Instead of charging interest to fellow Jews, lenders became partners with the debtors. Guaranteed against any loss, the lenders shared in part of the profit.

Don't call it interest. They don't.

53 First the sea parted so Moses and the Jews could cross it. Then the Jordan River stopped so Joshua and the Jews could cross it. Sounds like a rerun. Did someone get their stories crossed?

Sure. Some Christians could live with that approach to the Bible— admitting that some of the stories may have gotten twisted in the telling over the centuries. We see the same kind of thing with the Internet today—it can take only a few minutes to twist a news story into fact-killing gossip that goes viral.

Many Christians, however, would probably want to knock some sense into those other Christians.

The majority of Christians would likely say they trust the accuracy of the stories, insisting that God's Spirit guided the Bible writers and the compilers—making sure that God got his message across. (See Question 1, "What on earth do Christians mean when they say the Bible is 'inspired by God'"?)

As the story goes, Joshua and the Jewish refugees were about to cross into the Promised Land, today known as Israel. But they needed to wade across the Jordan River—during the spring flood season when "the water of the Jordan was going over its banks" (Joshua 3:15 NIRV).

There were no bridges. People generally crossed by wading on shallow fords—a bit like sandbars. But there was nothing shallow about the river on this particular day.

> When the priests who were carrying the ark came to the edge of the Jordan River and set foot in the water, the water stopped flowing from upstream. The water rose up like a dam as far away as the

city of Adam. . . . until the whole nation of Israel had crossed the Jordan River on dry ground.

Joshua 3:15–17

Yeah, right. What's not to believe?

Here's the surprise. The Jordan River has stopped many times in recorded history: 1267, 1546, 1834, 1906, 1927, and 1956.

The blockage in 1927 sounds like a page out of Joshua's story.

What happened that year, as in previous years, is because of the river's location. The Jordan River Valley marks the seam of a fault line. The valley separates two tectonic plates that are moving in roughly the same direction, but at different speeds.

In 1927, an earthquake shook loose the 150-foot (46-meter) cliffs near the ruins of the ancient city of Adam—possibly named for the Adam in the Bible. The rockslide blocked the river for twenty-one hours.

Adam lies about 20 miles (32 km) upstream from Jericho, on Jordan's side of the river. In Arabic, the ruin is known by the similar-sounding name of *Damiya*.

If that's what happened in Joshua's day, some wonder if the quake and aftershocks helped bring down the walls of nearby Jericho: "The troops shouted very loudly when they heard the blast of the rams' horns, and the wall collapsed" (Joshua 6:20).

54 Who's going to believe Jonah spent three days in the belly of a whale or some other sea critter?

From time to time over the last 100 years or so, some Christians have recycled a modern-day Jonah story. It's an urban legend.

We can trace it back to Joseph Pulitzer—of journalism's Pulitzer Prize fame. He published a story on April 12, 1896, in his prestigious *New York World* newspaper about a British whaler named James Bartley, who reportedly spent a day and a half inside a sperm whale.

As Mr. Bartley told it, his fellow crewmen sailing on the *Star of the East* around the Falkland Islands, near Argentina, caught the whale and cut Bartley free—unconscious and a shade lighter from marinating in gut juice.

In the follow-up stories that mark prize-winning journalism, reporters discovered that the ship's crew list did not include a Mr. Bartley. The ship's captain had died by the time reporters got to his house, but the captain's wife said Mr. Bartley was telling a fish tale, because he had never sailed with her husband.

Jonah, however, may not have had a close encounter with a whale. The Bible describes it only as "a big fish" (Jonah 1:17).

If the story happened exactly as it was told—and many Christians say they believe it did—perhaps Jonah didn't get a close enough look to tell whether it was a fish or a whale. He may not have seen anything but tonsils, teeth, and tongue. (Well, probably not tonsils. Neither fish nor whales have them.)

Maybe, as a landlubber, Jonah wouldn't have known a Mediterranean fin whale from a goldfish.

The fin whale, by the way, is the world's second largest animal, after the blue whale, which rarely swims into the Mediterranean. But even the blue can't usually swallow anything larger than a beach ball or a dinner plate. It takes a great white shark to swallow a grown man.

Christians who read Jonah's story as fact generally argue that God performs miracles. They say he created the universe, and he could easily have created a fish capable of carrying Jonah back to shore on a three-day cruise.

Other Christians say the story reads more like a fictional parable that's intended to teach a point. Supporting arguments:

- **Mental picture.** It's a vivid word picture that instantly captures the reader's attention with a prophet who "tried to run away from the Lord" (Jonah 1:3).
- **Wallop of an ending.** The story has an abrupt and shocking conclusion, much like the parables of Jesus. Jonah's warning of doom caused the city to repent, saving everyone. Yet Jonah was angry that his prediction didn't come true: he said, "I want to die" (Jonah 4:9).
- **A point to ponder.** Like many parables Jesus told, Jonah's story leaves readers to draw their own conclusions about what the purpose of the story is. The storyteller seems to point readers to the idea that God is the Lord of everyone, not just the Jews. And that God will forgive anyone who repents—even the worst of sinners. Assyrians had earned reputations as terrorists in those days. Art discovered in their palace ruins shows their soldiers impaling captives on sharpened fence posts.
- **No Jonah in Iraq.** Archaeologists have uncovered an extensive Assyrian library from Nineveh, the Iraqi city Jonah saved from destruction. There's no mention of Jonah in any document.
- **It doesn't read like prophecy.** Jonah's story has only one prediction, which doesn't come true. If it's a prophecy, it's one of a kind.

Christians who lobby against the theory that Jonah was just a parable remind us that Jonah shows up as a real person in Israel's history:

"Jonah, the prophet from Gath Hepher" (2 Kings 14:25).

This reference places him in the northern Jewish nation of Israel during the reign of Jeroboam (about 793–753 BC), when Assyrians ruled much of the Middle East.

Also, Jesus compared Jonah's three days in the belly of a fish to the three days he would spend in the grave: "Just as Jonah was in the belly of a huge fish for three days and three nights, so the Son of Man will be in the heart of the earth for three days and three nights" (Matthew 12:40).

As the argument goes, it would seem odd for Jesus to use a fictional story to illustrate such an important fact from his own story.

 55 So, the father of God's chosen people—the Jews—is Jacob, a jerk who cheated both his brother and his father, and then had to run for his life all the way to Turkey?

Jacob was a rascal in his younger days. That's putting it kindly. The dude stole his blind father's dying wish.

Isaac, Jacob's dad, thought he was about done breathing. So he wanted to give his oldest son, Esau, the traditional blessing—essentially a prayer for success.

Jacob dressed in Esau's clothes and conned Isaac into giving him the blessing instead.

Don't think Esau wasn't ticked: he said, "I'll kill my brother Jacob" (Genesis 27:41).

Earlier, Jacob had exploited Esau's hunger when Esau came home empty-handed after a hunt. Jacob refused to give him any of the soup he was cooking unless Esau agreed to a trade: "sell me your rights as firstborn" (Genesis 25:31). Firstborn sons got a double share of the family inheritance, along with the right to lead the extended family as alpha male.

Once Jacob got word that Esau intended to kill him, Jacob ran for his life.

He fled north out of their camp in Beersheba to what is now Turkey, where his mother's brother lived. Along the way he spent a night outside at a place he named Bethel (House of God), some seventy miles (113 km) north of his home—a two-day walk.

That's where the odd thing happened, in a vivid dream.

So far in the story, this dude is a dud.

Readers might be hoping God would crack open the earth and swallow him up.

Instead, God drenches him in promises:

- "I will give the land on which you are lying to you and your descendants."
- "Your descendants will be like the dust on the earth."
- "You will spread out to the west and to the east, to the north and to the south."
- "Through you and through your descendant every family on earth will be blessed."
- "Remember, I am with you and will watch over you wherever you go."
- "I will also bring you back to this land because I will not leave you until I do what I've promised you" (Genesis 28:13–15).

What was God thinking?

Was he simply honoring the blessing Jacob stole from Isaac: "Nations will be your servants and bow down to you. You will rule over your brothers, and they will kneel at your feet. Anyone who curses you will be cursed; anyone who blesses you will be blessed" (Genesis 27:29 CEV)?

Certainly God wasn't rewarding Jacob for exploiting his brother or for robbing his father. Yet those are the only two stories leading up to this scene—which is what makes the scene such a shocker.

There's no doubt about it, as the Bible writers tell the story. God did bless Jacob.

Jacob became the father of Israel's twelve tribes. Each one of Israel's tribes grew out of the extended families produced by Jacob's dozen sons.

Jews and Christians are left to puzzle over why God chose the likes of Jacob.

Many simply say God must have seen something in Jacob that we couldn't see in reading the story of Jacob's early years. Instead, God looked ahead and saw the man Jacob could and would become.

 56 Why did God handpick Saul to become Israel's first king only to trash him after Saul broke a nitpicking religious rule—an offense that seemed to warrant no more than a slap on the wrist?

It's true that God hired and fired Saul.

God hired. The Bible says God ordered the prophet Samuel to crown Saul as Israel's first king: "When Samuel noticed Saul, the Lord told him, 'There's the man I told you about. This man will govern my people'" (1 Samuel 9:17).

God fired. Years later—perhaps several decades, the Bible doesn't say when—God essentially fired him. Samuel delivered the news to Saul this way: "Because you rejected the word of the Lord, he rejects you as king" (1 Samuel 15:23).

Saul's offense. Samuel told Saul to kill everyone and everything when he went into battle against the Amalekites, a community of nomadic herders and raiders in the region. "Claim everything they have for God by destroying it" (1 Samuel 15:3).

Saul didn't. He brought back the best of the livestock.

When Samuel accused him of disobeying God, Saul's reply sounds a tad like an excuse he had worked up ahead of time: "The army took some of their belongings—the best sheep and cows were claimed for God—in order to sacrifice to the Lord your God in Gilgal" (1 Samuel 15:21).

Perhaps Saul figured he and his soldiers would get to keep the livestock. But even if Samuel insisted that they be sacrificed, Saul and the others would have gotten to eat part of these sacrifices of thanksgiving.

"To follow instructions is better than to sacrifice," Samuel said (1 Samuel 15:22).

"Samuel never saw Saul again the rest of his life, but he was sad for Saul" (1 Samuel 15:35 NCV).

Did God make a mistake in picking Saul in the first place? The Bible writer seems to say as much, quoting God: "I regret that I made Saul king" (1 Samuel 15:11).

Though Saul proved disappointing in the end, he served a purpose during his reign that's estimated at about forty years. He unified a loose coalition of family tribes into a nation with a powerful militia. Saul was a gifted commander-in-chief and a skilled, hands-on warrior himself. He was the kind of king that Israel seemed to need at the time, Bible experts say. He was no mistake.

But it may have been a big mistake for Samuel to continue to back him once Saul got too uppity to follow the instructions God gave him. That's the point at which God told Samuel to anoint the young shepherd David as Israel's next king.

It's a mystery why God rejected Saul so dramatically for what seems like a minor infraction. It's not as though Saul had sacrificed to idols. Yet when God's people were in their formative years— either the Jews or the Christians—Bible stories seem to paint the picture of God using stern measures to make sure his people knew that disobedience is serious business.

When Achan did the same kind of thing Saul did—essentially stealing from God—he wasn't just fired. He was burned. To death. (See Question 33, "Why did Joshua order a man and his entire family . . . ?")

And when the Christian movement was just getting started, a couple died after lying about their offering. (See Question 62. "Why would Peter condemn Ananias and Sapphira . . . ?")

Some Christians today say they wonder if these harsh measures had more to do with people than with God—perhaps writers telling the story and presuming God was behind it all since God is the boss of everything.

Probably most Christians, however, trust the stories as they are told. These Christians say they figure God had his reasons for doing what he did—and that he doesn't need to explain his reasons to us.

Still, we wonder. Curiosity is wired into us. Yet, at least for many, so is faith.

57 After God withdrew his Spirit from King Saul, "an evil spirit from the Lord tormented him." If God is good, what's he doing siccing an evil spirit on someone?

Bible scholars aren't sure what to make of this "evil spirit from the Lord" (1 Samuel 16:14), or how it affected King Saul.

Many Bible experts insist that God isn't a dealer when it comes to evil. He's the cop obsessed with getting the dealer off the streets: "There is no evil in him" (Psalm 92:15 NIRV).

Yet Bible writers often seem to finger God as the brains behind the evil muscle—the Godfather calling the shots.

- **Plotting disaster.** "Does disaster befall a city, unless the Lord has done it?" (Amos 3:6 NRSV).

- **Commissioning evil spirits.** "God sent an evil spirit to cause problems between Abimelech and citizens of Shechem" (Judges 9:23).
- **Recruiting liars.** "I saw the Lord sitting on his throne, and the entire army of heaven was standing near him on his right and his left. The Lord asked, 'Who will deceive Ahab so that he will attack and be killed?' . . . The Spirit answered, 'I will go out and be a spirit that tells lies through the mouths of all of Ahab's prophets.' The Lord said . . . 'Go and do it'" (1 Kings 22:19–20, 22).

Here are some of the theories that Bible experts offer to explain what was going on with Saul.

The Bible writer got it wrong. Many Jews in Bible times taught that God controlled everything. If something good happened, it was God rewarding the person. If something bad happened, it was God punishing the person.

This is a warped idea that many Bible experts say the story of Job refutes. Job was a good guy, but rotten things happened to him.

Jesus also refuted the idea when he told his disciples that a man who was born blind wasn't blinded because God wanted to punish him or his parents: "He was born blind so that God could show what he can do for him" (John 9:3). Then Jesus healed the man.

Perhaps, some students of the Bible say, the Bible writers or later editors made the link to God instead of linking Saul's troubled soul to his busted relationship with God and to God's prophet Samuel. (See Question 56, "Why did God handpick Saul . . . ?")

Saul's advisors got it wrong. The king's advisors were the ones who seemed to have made the diagnosis. "Saul's officials told him, 'An evil spirit from God is tormenting you'" (1 Samuel 16:15). The Bible writer was simply reporting what they said.

Saul was depressed. He had every reason to feel troubled, dark-hearted, and hopeless. He had disobeyed God by taking livestock from a conquered nation. So God rejected him.

Saul had taken quite the plunge: from a king who ruled with God's backing to a king on whom God turned his back.

Saul ruled alone. He couldn't even get advice from Israel's top prophet Samuel, who refused to ever meet with him again.

The Bible writer didn't have a medical degree and didn't recognize the symptoms of depression. But he did, perhaps correctly, attribute Saul's condition to a spiritual problem. One Bible version translates 1 Samuel 16:15: "A tormenting spirit from God is troubling you" (NLT). *The Message* puts it this way: "This awful tormenting depression from God is making your life miserable."

Whatever Saul's affliction was, music therapy seemed to work—a least for a stretch of time. David's soothing strums from a lyre, an instrument that looks like a harp that got wet and shrunk, soothed Saul's soul.

58 Why should anyone believe there's an evil spirit called the devil? He's a no-show in the entire Jewish Bible, which Christians call the Old Testament.

It's true that many Jewish scholars say they don't see the devil showing up as a supernatural being in their Bible.

They say that Satan is an idea that gradually developed after the Old Testament was written—and that Jews probably picked it up during their exile in what is now Iraq and Iran, about 500 years before Jesus. Persians were big on the idea of good versus evil.

That surprises many Christians, because they read about Satan in the Old Testament. So they ask, what about . . .

- the snake that told Eve, if she ate the forbidden fruit, "you'll be like God" (Genesis 3:5).
- Job's nemesis, "Satan," who told God if Job faced calamity, "I bet he'll curse you to your face" (Job 1:11).

But *Satan* is a Hebrew word that simply means "enemy" or "accuser." It can refer to anyone who takes a stand against someone else. Sometimes in the Bible *Satan* actually refers to God.

We can see it pretty clearly when we compare two versions of the same story reported in two different books of the Bible.

- "Satan attempted to attack Israel by provoking David to count the Israelites" (1 Chronicles 21:1).
- "The Lord became angry with Israel again, so he provoked David to turn against Israel. He said, 'Go, count Israel and Judah'" (2 Samuel 24:1).

So in Job's story, which some say is fiction, Satan could simply be a prosecuting-attorney-type angel.

As for the snake, the Genesis writer never said it was anything more than a talking snake. We have to wait for a Christian who was probably writing 100 years after the birth of Jesus to link the snake to the devil: "That ancient snake, named Devil and Satan, the deceiver of the whole world" (Revelation 12:9).

For most Christians, Jesus offers the strongest evidence for believing in the devil.

- Jesus talked with the devil during his forty-day temptation: "Go away, Satan!" (Matthew 4:10).
- Jesus taught about Satan: "I watched Satan fall from heaven" (Luke 10:18).
- Jesus cast out demons controlled by "Satan, the prince of demons" (Matthew 12:24 NLT).

Paul, the apostle who wrote almost half the books of the New Testament, spoke of the spiritual battles we all face: "This is for keeps, a life-or-death fight to the finish against the Devil and all his angels" (Ephesians 6:12 THE MESSAGE).

Most Christians say they can relate to what Paul said. They feel a spiritual tug-of-war going on in their lives—with a tenacious pull toward darkness and the forbidden.

They also tend to acknowledge that some people even today are demon possessed, and that priests, missionaries, and pastors aren't exaggerating when they describe exorcisms they've conducted.

59 Why did God strike a man dead for nothing more than trying to protect Israel's most sacred relic— the ark of the covenant, a chest that held the Ten Commandments?

Neither of the two Bible writers who reported Uzzah's sad story bothered to explain such a harsh penalty: "The Lord became angry with Uzzah and killed him for reaching for the ark" (1 Chronicles 13:10).

Scholars, however, say they've found some context clues to why Uzzah died while helping King David move the ark to Jerusalem.

Uzzah touched the untouchable. God had ordered that only members of the priestly tribe of Levi—the Levites—could carry holy objects such as the ark.

And even those Levites "must never touch the holy things, or they will die" (Numbers 4:15). They had to use poles to carry the ark.

As well-intentioned as Uzzah might have been, some scholars say, he should have known the laws about the ark—especially since it had been stored and guarded in his father's house "for a full 20 years" (1 Samuel 7:2 NIRV).

The ark didn't belong on an oxcart. It's a mystery why the Jews decided to carry the ark to Jerusalem on an oxcart. Maybe it's because that's how the Philistines returned it to Israel after capturing it in a battle: "Hitch the cows to the cart. . . . Take the ark of the Lord, and put it on the cart" (1 Samuel 6:7–8).

David koshered up the transportation details the second go-round: "The Levites carried God's ark on their shoulders. They used poles as Moses had commanded according to the Lord's instructions" (1 Chronicles 15:15).

David didn't consult God. When David had a big decision to make, the Bible often says "David asked the Lord" (2 Samuel 5:19). But on his first attempt to move the ark, he merely consulted "with every officer who commanded a regiment or battalion" (1 Chronicles 13:1).

Still, it seems odd to kill Uzzah for either a well-intended "oops" or for David's mistakes.

Some Christians say they wonder if there are other reasons the writer said God killed Uzzah. Maybe there's more to the story than we know. Perhaps Uzzah did something else that warranted the death penalty.

Or maybe Uzzah died accidentally, possibly crushed by the ark or the oxcart. And maybe the writer merely presumed God arranged the execution. Since many Jews seemed to believe that God controlled everything that happened—good and bad—it may have seemed a logical presumption.

60 Jesus said we shouldn't judge one another, so why do Christians do it so much?

When we live life by a stack of rules—as many Christians do—it's tempting to call others on it when they break one of our rules.

It's also tempting to vote for laws that require everyone to obey our rules.

What many Christians want is heaven on earth—or as close to it as we can get.

We'd like a Christian nation, at least. Yet we can't seem to agree on what's Christian and what's not—or how best to nudge others in the direction we'd like them to go.

Should we nudge the non-Christians by simply living the Golden Rule that Jesus taught, and then keep our mouths shut about judgment and criticism? "Here is a simple, rule-of-thumb guide for behavior: Ask yourself what you want people to do for *you*, then grab the initiative and do it for *them*. Add up God's Law and Prophets and this is what you get" (Matthew 7:12 THE MESSAGE).

Or should we add a dash of aggression to the love potion?

- picket
- boycott
- ban books
- contact our congressional representatives

Frankly, many Christians say it's a bit hard for them to know what to do because Bible writers seem to give them mixed messages.

Don't judge others

Jesus put it this way in the Sermon on the Mount: "Do not judge others. Then you will not be judged. You will be judged in the same way you judge others. . . . You look at the bit of sawdust in your friend's eye. But you pay no attention to the piece of wood in your own eye" (Matthew 7:1–3 NIRV).

Jesus practiced what he preached when a herd of law-abiding Jews asked him what they should do with a woman caught in the act of adultery—a death-by-stoning offense according to Jewish law.

Jesus said, "The person who is sinless should be the first to throw a stone at her" (John 8:7).

The apostle Paul gave this advice to Christians in Rome: "Every time you criticize someone, you condemn yourself. It takes one to know one. Judgmental criticism of others is a well-known way of escaping detection in your own crimes" (Romans 2:1 THE MESSAGE).

Go ahead, judge others

On the other hand, Paul condemned a church in Greece for not passing judgment on a church member.

> I can hardly believe the report about the sexual immorality going on among you—something that even pagans don't do. I am told that a man in your church is living in sin with his stepmother. You are so proud of yourselves, but you should be mourning in sorrow and shame. And you should remove this man from your fellowship.
>
> 1 Corinthians 5:1–2 NLT

Paul went so far as to set up procedures for passing judgment on church leaders: "Don't pay attention to an accusation against a spiritual leader unless it is supported by two or three witnesses. Reprimand those leaders who sin. Do it in front of everyone so that the other leaders will also be afraid" (1 Timothy 5:19–20).

So, as the Bible tells it, there's a time to speak up and a time to shut up.

Christians in the early church seemed to reserve their criticism for fellow believers. When it came to folks outside the church, they seemed okay with letting God handle the judging.

Yet many Christians today feel compelled to take a firm and public stand against evil. So much so that the non-Christians they target say they sense in Christianity more hatred than love.

Many Christians would admit that they need to work on that. When Christians speak the truth—especially in judgment—they say we should consider taking Paul's advice: "Speak the truth in love" (Ephesians 4:15 NIRV).

Or don't speak at all.

61 The Bible says if you raise a child right, the kid will grow up nice and religious. I know some pastors' kids who didn't turn out quite like that.

Here's the proverb: "Teach your children right from wrong, and when they are grown they will still do right" (Proverbs 22:6 CEV).

Funny thing about pastors' kids, they seem to act out worse than your average kid.

Maybe it just seems that way because they're in the spotlight. Or because we expect more of them. I mean, goodness gracious, they are pastors' kids.

The apostle Paul said men who couldn't control their own kids shouldn't be pastors: "They must see that their children are obedient and always respectful. If they don't know how to control their own families, how can they look after God's people?" (1 Timothy 3:4–5 CEV).

Spoken like a bachelor, some say of Paul—who never married.

One reason some say pastors' kids are a little more wild than other kids is because pastors are gone from home so much: meetings, counseling, weddings, funerals, sermon prep, on call 24/7.

As for the proverb, most Bible experts say it's not a promise. It's an observation.

The book of Proverbs is a collection of wise sayings—observations and insights that Jewish elders wanted to pass along to their young men. It's an ancient version of lessons from the school of hard knocks, from an experienced generation to the up-and-coming rookie generation.

The writer of this particular proverb has noticed that children raised in good homes by good parents more often than not tend to turn out well.

Lessons we learn in our childhood travel with us throughout our lives. Some lessons for the better. Some for the worse.

The sage behind this proverb seems to be encouraging young fathers to teach their kids lessons for the better.

62 Why would Peter condemn Ananias and Sapphira to death for exaggerating their donation? Why not thank them instead?

Any way you slice it, this story sounds like overkill. Literally.

Ananias and Sapphira did not deserve to die. Not if what is reported in the Bible is all there is to the story. That's certainly how most folks seem to feel about it.

This forces Bible experts to read between the lines as they search for clues to the question "Why did this philanthropic couple have to die?"

Scholars start their quest by reading the story just before the one about Ananias and Sapphira—to get the context.

As the story goes, believers in the new Christian movement were looking out for each other. Some sold land or other possessions and gave the money to the apostles to distribute among poor believers.

Joseph, a man from Cyprus, sold some of his land "and turned the money over to the apostles" (Acts 4:37). In appreciation, the apostles gave Joseph a new name: Barnabas, which means "encourager." This may have been the same Barnabas who later traveled with the apostle Paul on his first missionary trip.

From the Barnabas story, the Bible writer jumped immediately to the story of Ananias and Sapphira—as though this couple wanted in on some of that high praise that Barnabas got.

Maybe they could get their names upgraded, too. Ananias, which means "God is merciful," might become Eli, "Exalted." Sapphira, meaning "Good," might become Eudokia, "Goodwill."

The couple sold a piece of property. They gave *some* of the money to the apostles, but said they gave *all* the money.

The lie feels like it belongs in the category of cheating on taxes, exaggerating on a résumé, or telling your blind date that you're a corporate office manager—when what you really manage is keeping the offices clean. The fib doesn't feel like it belongs in the category of first-degree murder, warranting the death penalty.

When Ananias appears before the apostle Peter, possibly to deliver the money, Peter's reaction seems to shock Ananias to death. Perhaps, some speculate, it sparked a heart attack or a stroke.

Peter asked, "Ananias, why did you let Satan fill you with the idea that you could deceive the Holy Spirit? You've held back some of the money you received for the land. While you had the land, it was your own. After it was sold, you could have done as you pleased with the money. So how could you do a thing like this? You didn't lie to people but to God!"

Acts 5:3–4

Apparently with Peter's words still ringing in his ears, Ananias "dropped dead."

Ananias's wife, Sapphira, showed up later.

Peter, instead of telling her that her husband has died, asks her a question:

"Did you sell the land for that price?"

She answered, "Yes, that was the price."

Then Peter said to her, "How could you and your husband agree to test the Lord's Spirit? Those who buried your husband are standing at the door, and they will carry you outside for burial."

Immediately, she dropped dead in front of Peter.

Acts 5:8–10

Some Bible experts speculate that it wasn't God who killed the couple. It was shock.

Given the miracles they may have seen the apostles perform in God's name, hearing the lead apostle accuse them of lying to God could possibly stop a heart. That's one theory.

Yet many Bible experts say the story reads as though the writer wasn't blaming some natural cause for the deaths, but was pointing the finger at God. Otherwise, Peter would not have been able to predict the death of Sapphira.

Whether or not God caused the deaths remains a matter of debate.

If God did kill the couple, the question "Why?" remains a mystery.

One popular guess is that this was the first time on record that Christians tested God by presuming that the Christian movement was more about what the people were doing than about what God was doing. So at this pivotal moment in history, God took stern measures to assure everyone that, in fact, he was on the job and that Christianity was not a religious movement driven by humans and their money. It was a movement powered by God's Spirit.

 63 Why would a thinking person believe the story that the reason we have so many languages is because God punished people for building the Tower of Babel?

It's not clear what the people did that upset God. The most common guess among scholars is that the people got too big for their britches: "Let's make ourselves famous" (Genesis 11:4 THE MESSAGE). Apparently, they intended to do that by building a tower that reached into the heavens, where some said the gods lived.

God's response: "Let us go down there and mix up their language so that they won't understand each other" (Genesis 11:7). "This is why it was named Babel, because there the Lord turned the language of the whole earth into babble" (Genesis 11:9).

Scholars identify the location as Babylon—think "babble on." With today's map, we would find it in southern Iraq, where many scholars say human civilization began.

The Bible isn't the only ancient writing that tells about a god mixing up human languages. A similar story shows up in the writings of the world's first-known civilization—Sumer, in what is now southern Iraq:

> Enki . . . leader of the gods
> changed the language people spoke,

bringing confusion into it
by turning one language into many.

From the Sumerian story called
Enmerkar and the Lord of Aratta

Some folks say they take the Bible story literally, as history. Others, not so much.

Some say they read this as a way of mocking earlier Middle Eastern stories, such as the one from Sumer, by arguing that if any such thing happened, it was God who made it happen.

Still others say they wonder if the writer was treating a mystery of history the way scientists treat modern-day mysteries. They start with a fact, such as a mountain. Then they work up theories about what might have produced that mountain.

As this theory goes, the Bible writer started with the fact that people in his day spoke many languages, depending on where they lived. So he theorized that God made the centralized human race speak different languages, and that people scattered abroad by language groups.

The question Christians grapple with is whether or not this story was intended as history or as something else—perhaps as a way of pushing back at the claim that a Sumerian god was the source of human language.

64 Why did God introduce himself to Moses by speaking from a burning bush, of all things?

It made an impression on Moses.

He was minding his own business, tending his father-in-law's sheep near the foot of Mount Sinai. Suddenly, "The angel of the

Lord appeared to him in a blazing fire from the middle of a bush. Moses stared in amazement. Though the bush was engulfed in flames, it didn't burn up" (Exodus 3:2 NLT).

Most Bible scholars say "angel of the Lord" actually refers to God himself. *Angel* means "messenger." As the theory goes, this fire may simply have been the form God took to personally deliver his message to Moses.

Perhaps a bush was the closest object to Moses that God could use to engage the shepherd's curiosity without triggering a heart attack.

Students of the Bible have speculated about what kind of fire could appear to burn a bush. One guess: St. Elmo's fire. It's a weather phenomenon sometimes caused by thunderstorms. A strong electrical field can make the tips of objects seem to glow: grass, branches, and leaves.

Even the tips of horns on cattle.

Holy cow.

Some scholars say the fire was real. They say the fact that the bush didn't burn was a foreshadowing of other nature-busting miracles to come, especially during the ten plagues of Egypt: the Nile River turning to blood, dust balls turning into gnats, firstborn children suddenly dying.

Others say the fire wasn't physical at all. They call the fiery bush a *theophany*, "an appearance of God." The fire may have been no more physical than a vision, a dream, or the celestial form Jesus seemed to take during his transfiguration: "Jesus' appearance changed in front of them. His face became as bright as the sun and his clothes as white as light" (Matthew 17:2).

God glows.

So it seems, if we take literally some Bible descriptions of him.

Pillar of fire. "By day the Lord went ahead of them in a column of smoke to lead them on their way. By night he went ahead of them in a column of fire to give them light so that they could travel by day or by night" (Exodus 13:21).

Falling fire. "All of Mount Sinai was covered with smoke because the Lord had come down on it in fire" (Exodus 19:18).

Fire on the mountain. "To the Israelites, the glory of the Lord looked like a raging fire on top of the mountain" (Exodus 24:17).

In the spotlight. "Then I saw what he looked like from the waist up. He looked like glowing bronze with fire all around it. From the waist down, he looked like fire. A bright light surrounded him" (Ezekiel 1:27).

Light of heaven. "There will be no more night, and they will not need any light from lamps or the sun because the Lord God will shine on them" (Revelation 22:5).

Why would God choose light as a way of representing himself to Moses and other people?

The Bible writers don't say. But light is a good thing and darkness scary, especially in that age before electricity. Light became a wonderful, upbeat symbol for God—making him out to be a bit like the cowboy in the white hat instead of the raggedy cowpoke in the black hat.

Linking God to light, poets praised him with lyrics like these:

- "The Lord is my light and my salvation. Who is there to fear?" (Psalm 27:1).
- "Blessed are the people who know how to praise you. They walk in the light of your presence, O Lord" (Psalm 89:15).
- "Darkness covers the earth. Thick darkness spreads over the nations. But I will rise and shine on you. My glory will appear over you. Nations will come to your light. Kings will come to the brightness of your new day" (Isaiah 60:2–3 NIRV).

Light has a magnet-like power to attract. Vacationers can stare for hours at a campfire. Bugs can swarm all night long around outdoor lights.

And once upon a time, as the Bible tells it, Moses was drawn by a light in the wilderness.

65 Why do preachers tell people they have to tithe 10 percent of their income, when tithing is one of many Jewish laws that Christians throughout the centuries have said is obsolete?

Churches today, at least in the United States, get most of their money from tithing. When it comes to raising money, tithing works.

"If it ain't broke, don't fix it." That's one reason church leaders might not want to throw the tithing baby out with what some say is its theologically stinky bath water.

Some scholars—especially church historians—argue that tithing is more Jewish than Christian. Tithing is law in the Jewish Bible, which Christians call the Old Testament. But tithing is a no-show in the Christian add-on: the New Testament.

As far as New Testament writers tell it, Christians weren't asked to give 10 percent of their income. They were asked to give offerings.

- "Every Sunday each of you make an offering and put it in safekeeping. Be as generous as you can. When I get there you'll have it ready, and I won't have to make a special appeal" (1 Corinthians 16:1 THE MESSAGE).

- "Churches in Macedonia . . . gave as much as they could afford and even more, simply because they wanted to" (2 Corinthians 8:1, 3 CEV).

Jews, on the other hand, were bound by law to give "One-tenth of what comes from the land. . . . Every tenth head of cattle or sheep" (Leviticus 27:30, 32). Tithing was just one of the hundreds of specific laws that God's people were expected to observe.

New Testament Christians taught that Jesus rendered those laws obsolete: "When God speaks of a 'new' covenant, it means he has made the first one obsolete. It is now out of date and will soon disappear" (Hebrews 8:13 NLT).

Church historians shock many Christians with reports like these:

- The apostle Paul collected offerings, but never asked anyone to tithe.
- Martin Luther (1483–1546), founder of the Protestant movement, didn't tithe.
- John Calvin (1509–1564), theological father of many Baptists and Presbyterians, didn't tithe.
- John Wesley (1703–1791), founder of the Methodist church, didn't tithe. He did, however, die broke because he gave his wealth away.
- Christian ministers didn't preach a single sermon on tithing until the 1800s, according to Dr. Paul Bassett, professor emeritus of the history of Christianity from Nazarene Theological Seminary and a former advisor to *Christianity Today* magazine.

A tax cut is what turned American churches toward tithing, historians say.

Taxes funded American churches, as they still do in many countries. Early Americans argued that religion was important enough to deserve public support. But in 1833, states started rescinding the religious tax.

Churches scrambling for ways to fill the fiscal gap tried lots of fund-raising techniques.

Renting pews, for example—"Will that be cash or charge?"

But the most effective fund-raising technique was to adopt the Jewish tradition—and portray it as one of the never-expiring laws of God, such as the Ten Commandments.

It had quite an effect on congregations when the minister quoted one prophet in particular:

- **Reward for tithing.** "Bring one-tenth of your income into the storehouse so that there may be food in my house. Test me in this way. . . . See if I won't open the windows of heaven for you and flood you with blessings" (Malachi 3:10). *Many preachers said the church was God's "storehouse." Some preachers promised that God would reward people who tithed. Some still make that promise.*
- **Don't cheat God.** "Should people cheat God? Yet you have cheated me. . . . You have cheated me of the tithes and offerings due to me" (Malachi 3:8 NLT).

Today, most churches ask their people to tithe.

Some church historians suggest a compromise that they say would better reflect early Christian teaching and tradition: Invite Christians to give offerings. Suggest 10 percent as a reasonable guideline for those who can afford it, acknowledging that some can't and others can do far more. But don't sell the 10 percent tithe as God's law for Christians, when the Bible presents it as an obsolete law for Jews.

Many pastors would resist this, arguing that the Old Testament is every bit as much God's Word as is the New Testament.

 66 Elijah went to heaven in a chariot of fire? Doesn't it sound suspicious that the only witness was his successor, Elisha?

Actually, it was a whirlwind. And the Bible says a group of fifty prophets knew Elijah was about to leave the planet.

As elderly Elijah and his young apprentice prophet, Elisha, walked toward the Jordan River, some of the other prophets pulled young Elisha aside and asked a question: "Do you know that the Lord is going to take your master from you today?" (2 Kings 2:3). "Yes, I know," he said.

Old Elijah intended to cross the river alone and somehow meet his Maker on the other side, in what is now the Arab country of Jordan. But Elisha insisted on crossing the river with him.

What young Elisha witnessed on that walk is anyone's guess. The Bible writer—who some scholars say finally wrote down a story that had been passed along by word of mouth for centuries—describes it this way: "As they continued walking and talking, a chariot of fire and horses of fire separated the two of them, and Elijah ascended in a whirlwind into heaven" (2 Kings 2:11 NRSV).

Readers looking for a rational explanation might suggest that the writer, using poetic flair, painted natural events with a little extra color:

- lightning becomes fiery chariots
- a tornado or a massive dust storm whipped up by an approaching frontal system becomes a heaven-sent whirlwind
- Elijah's disappearance into the tornado or windstorm becomes a celestial airlift.

Few scholars would buy into that theory because there's no hint of clouds, blowing sand, or wind.

We'd find more scholars inclined to portray the story as a legend that got exaggerated over the passing generations.

Many others, however, say they read the story more like a news report from ancient history.

God is often associated with fire. (See Question 64 about Moses and the burning bush.)

Ditto for God and whirlwinds:

- "Then the Lord answered Job out of the whirlwind" (Job 38:1 NRSV).

- "Terrify them with your storms" (Psalm 83:15 CEV).
- "The Lord's anger bursts out like a storm, a whirlwind that swirls down on the heads of the wicked" (Jeremiah 23:19 NLT).

Still others say they read the story as history with a dash of symbolism. Perhaps, for example, Elisha saw a sky full of celestial beings, which he described as "Israel's chariot and horses!" (2 Kings 2:12). Or maybe he was referring to Elijah himself, portraying him as stronger than all the armies of Israel.

Whatever Elisha saw, as the Bible tells the tale, it was remarkable. It ended the earthly life of Elijah, and it wasn't a felony.

Many Jews came to believe that one day Elijah would return as an advance man for the Messiah: "I'm going to send you the prophet Elijah before that very terrifying day of the Lord comes" (Malachi 4:5).

Jesus said John the Baptist fulfilled that prophecy: "John is the Elijah who was to come" (Matthew 11:14).

Yet New Testament writers also report that Elijah came back at the transfiguration of Jesus, shortly before the crucifixion: "Suddenly, Moses and Elijah appeared to them and were talking with Jesus" (Matthew 17:3).

 67 Why did the prophet Elisha invoke God's name to put a curse on boys for calling him "Baldy," and is that why bears killed them?

That is one weird story all right. But the writer never does come out and say God sicced the bears on the boys. For all we know, it could have been a bizarre coincidence.

Yet given the widespread Jewish belief that God controlled everything, some scholars argue that the writer probably presumed God prodded the bears.

Here's the entire story:

> Elisha went up to Bethel. On the way some boys came out of the city and made fun of him. They said to him, "Go up too, you baldhead! Go up too, you baldhead!" Elisha turned around, looked at them, and put a curse on them in the name of the Lord. Then two mother bears came out of the woods and tore forty-two of the boys to pieces.
>
> 2 Kings 2:23–24 NCV

Okay, that sounds harsh.

And it sounds like Elisha could have made excellent use of happy pills.

Was this a case of a grumpy old man with more ego than hair sentencing little kids to death for doing what little kids do naturally: tease, taunt, and rebel?

The writer didn't bother to say.

Bible experts call our attention to some clues in the story that might add a little insight.

The word describing the boys could also refer to young men, including teenagers and young adults. It's used that way elsewhere in the Bible.

"Go up too," may refer to Elisha's mentor, Elijah—who had just left the planet, carried into the heavens by a whirlwind and a chariot of fire. If that's what the boys were saying, Elisha might have taken their taunt a bit like we would take "Drop dead!" or worse, "Go to hell."

Still, if bears mauled everyone who told someone else to go to hell, rush hour wouldn't be so bad.

One educated guess is that this story is intended—perhaps a bit like a parable—to send a message about the fate of Elisha's homeland: the northern Jewish nation of Israel.

The Jewish people disrespected God, just as the Jewish boys disrespected God's prophet.

By unleashing a curse on the boys, Elisha was painting a bloodred vivid portrait of what God had warned would happen:

If you keep rebelling against me . . . I'll send wild animals to attack you, and they will gobble down your children.

Leviticus 26:21–22 cev

Assyrian invaders from what is now Iraq overran Israel in 722 BC, roughly a generation after Elisha. The invasion force wiped the Jewish nation off the political map and resettled the land with Assyrian pioneers.

68 Why would God order the death penalty for kids who hit their parents or who do nothing more than speak disrespectfully to them?

Imagine trying to get this dynamic duo of laws through the Supreme Court:

- "Anyone who dishonors father or mother must be put to death. Such a person is guilty of a capital offense" (Leviticus 20:9 NLT).
- "Suppose someone has a very stubborn son. He doesn't obey his father and mother. And he won't listen to them when they try to correct him. . . . Then all of the people in his town will put him to death by throwing stones at him" (Deuteronomy 21:18, 21 NIRV).

Most Bible experts don't seem to know what to do with these laws. They simply report them as fact and move on to the next paragraph in the Bible.

Some Bible experts, however, try to soften the laws—regardless of the fact that death by stoning is always going to leave a mark. Arguments some use to help justify the laws:

- The disobedient kids were repeat offenders.
- The law protected kids from their angry parents by requiring the community to condemn and, if necessary, execute the children.
- Chronically disobedient children could threaten the survival of the family, in a day when families depended almost exclusively on each other.
- Perhaps the laws were symbolic—a way of emphasizing the seriousness of the sin. Maybe the kids were saved by a substitute offering, a bit like paying a fine. Some scholars say they see the possibility of this implied by a law prohibiting such ransom for murderers: "Never accept a cash payment in exchange for the life of a convicted murderer" (Numbers 35:31).

Yet to some Christians, laws that strike the fear of God into children seem to suggest that God may have had an editor with parenting issues.

Passages like these do, in fact, make some Christians wonder if the less palatable laws attributed to God really did come from him.

Other Christians say they have no doubt the Bible is genuinely God-approved through and through, and that when it comes to tough passages like these, they give God the benefit of the doubt—figuring they'll understand it by and by, when all the facts become known.

69 Did God really clobber Egypt with ten plagues? The poisoned Nile River turning red, swarms of bugs, epidemics, three days of darkness—it all sounds over the top.

The story does not sound realistic. That's what makes it extraordinary—a Bible headliner.

Here's the short version of what happened: Jews migrated to the Nile River Valley in Egypt to escape a seven-year drought in their homeland. Egyptians enslaved them. God sent Moses to ask Egypt's king to free the Jews. When the king refused, Moses twisted his arm with plagues. It took ten plagues, from autumn to springtime, to convince the king to give in and free the Jews.

Christians generally approach this story in one of three ways:

- God can do anything—including everything in this story. Easy peasy for the Creator of the universe.
- God can do anything, but did he really do everything in this story? Maybe the story got a bit bigger in the retelling, from one generation to the next.
- God created the laws of nature for a reason. Perhaps he put them to good use by orchestrating the ten plagues.

This third option has spawned a popular theory, which as far as many Christians are concerned is more intriguing than believable. Yet many folks wonder if there might be at least some truth to parts of the theory.

As the theory goes, the ten plagues weren't isolated disasters. They were a domino effect of many natural disasters—starting with the annual autumn flooding of the Nile River and ending with springtime harvest.

1. Nile River turns to blood. The Nile flooded almost every fall, as rain and snowmelt from the heart of Africa poured into the tributaries that fed the Nile. Stagnant water from swamps upriver could have swept into the flood, releasing toxic algae bacteria. Think red tide. It usually happens at sea, turning the water red.

2. Frog infestation. Frogs flee the poisoned water.

3. Insect swarms. Insects could have bred in the pools of receding water after the flood.

4. Flies. Stable flies often lay eggs in wet material such as straw or even in decaying material such as dead frogs.

5. Livestock disease. Farm animals can get anthrax from contaminated water. They can also catch diseases such as African horse sickness or the bluetongue virus from insects.

6. Boils. The bite of a stable fly can produce blisters or boils. So can eating meat contaminated with anthrax.

7. Hail. It's still a common threat in Egypt.

8. Locusts. These aggressive grasshopper-looking critters are still a common threat in spite of modern pesticides. Billions descended on North Africa in 2004. And in 2013, billions more infested half of the African nation of Madagascar—the worst swarm there since the 1950s.

9. Three days of darkness. Egyptians today call it *Khamsin*, which is Arabic for "fifty days." It's a hot blast of wind from the Sahara Desert. It can blow in anytime from March through May, filling the air with sand that can block the sun for days.

10. Death of firstborn. This is perhaps the weakest link in the theory that the plagues were a string of natural disasters. Some theorize that the oldest children died because it was custom to give the oldest child extra everything—including meat and grain possibly contaminated by the effects of the Nile flood. But that wouldn't explain the death of the firstborn animals.

Another plague theory is that the eruption of a volcano on the island of Thera, north of Egypt, released gasses that turned the Nile River red.

That happened in the African country of Cameroon in 1986, killing 1,700 people and 3,500 livestock. A pocket of magma released gasses into the water, creating carbonic acid that turned the water rust red. The gasses rose into a massive cloud of carbon dioxide that suffocated the people.

As far-fetched as the plague story sounds, some of the same plagues seem to show up in an ancient Egyptian document: *The Admonitions of Ipuwer,* written in about 1200 BC—the same century when many scholars say Moses lived. Other scholars put Moses 200 years earlier.

Exodus Plague	Egyptian Plague
"All the water in the river turned into blood" (7:20).	"The river is blood."
"There was blood everywhere in Egypt" (7:21).	"Blood is everywhere."
"All over Egypt the hail . . . destroyed every tree in the fields" (9:25).	"Trees are down."
"The flax and the barley were ruined, because the barley had formed heads and the flax was in bloom" (9:31).	"The barley crop has been destroyed."
"There was loud crying throughout Egypt because in every house someone had died" (12:30).	"People who bury their dead are everywhere."

70 God killed 70,000 Jews because King David took a census? What's wrong with counting warm bodies, and why would God punish innocent folks for something their king did?

This bizarre story shows up in two books of the Bible: 2 Samuel 24 and 1 Chronicles 21.

Neither story makes sense. The writers left out important details.

Imagine reading a news story about someone getting sentenced to death, but not telling why. That's what is going on in this story.

As both Bible writers tell it, David did something wrong. We don't know what. Angry, God somehow provoked David to take a census. In the Chronicles version, the provoker was *Satan*, the Hebrew word for "Accuser." Many scholars say that in this context, "Accuser" could refer to God.

Apparently, something was wrong about taking the census, too. When David ordered his top general to take the census, Joab replied, "Why do you wish to make Israel guilty of this sin?" (1 Chronicles 21:3).

Again, scholars can't figure out what Joab seemed to know right away—that the census David ordered wasn't kosher.

One of many long-shot guesses: it was a pride thing. David wanted to show off the size of his army and perhaps take credit for the military victories God had given him.

Tougher questions:

• Why would God provoke David to do something wrong?
• Why would God kill 70,000 Jews for David's crime?

Short answer: God knows and he's not talking.

Some scholars argue that though God isn't evil, he can give evil people an opportunity to put their evil on display. That way, when the evildoer gets what evildoers get—punished—people looking on might make the connection that God punishes sinners.

As for the Jews dying because of David's sin, many scholars insist that whatever sin David committed, the Jews committed it as well.

If Israel's sin was pride in themselves as a can-do nation instead of pride in God as their can-do defender, they were as guilty as David. Still, is an overabundance of self-esteem a capital offense?

Maybe the crime was some other sin, such as idolatry or child sacrifices that many scholars say were common in the region.

No one knows for sure what the sin was.

Yet most Christians say they trust the justice of God, and they figure that if we knew the answers to all the questions in this story, we would agree that God did the right thing.

Some scholars say they wonder if the story is more about God's grace than about punishment. After all, the story ends with David buying the land that would become home to Israel's worship center: the Jerusalem temple.

To end the plague, David bought a ridgetop threshing floor and "built an altar for the Lord there and sacrificed burnt offerings" (1 Chronicles 21:26). That rock-solid ground became Israel's place of worship. Born of sin, it became Israel's most holy place—the home of God, and the way to forgiveness.

Some Christians say they wonder if the story is more symbolic than literal—perhaps pointing to God as Israel's savior. Some details read like subtle clues pointing to other Bible stories of God saving his people.

- The angel of the Lord that appeared to David may be the writer's way of pointing back to the angel of the Lord who told Joshua, on the brink of invading what is now Israel, "Take off your sandals because this place where you are standing is holy" (Joshua 5:15).

• David bought the temple land from a farmer threshing grain. Israel's hero, Gideon, was threshing grain when an angel showed up and said, "You will rescue Israel" (Judges 6:14).

71 The Bible says if parents don't beat their children, they don't love them: "Those who spare the rod of discipline hate their children." Really?

To spank or not to spank. That is the question raised by Proverbs 13:24 (NLT).

Does the Bible order up a good spanking on kids misbehaving?

• "Foolishness is firmly attached to a child's heart. Spanking will remove it far from him" (Proverbs 22:15).
• "Do not hesitate to discipline a child. If you spank him, he will not die. Spank him yourself, and you will save his soul from hell" (Proverbs 23:13–14).
• "A spanking and a warning produce wisdom, but an undisciplined child disgraces his mother" (Proverbs 29:15).

Bible experts don't generally agree on much of anything. But most do seem to agree that the wise old men of Proverbs, offering their advice from life's school of hard knocks, were talking about giving kids a wallop of an attitude adjustment—as needed.

Scholars say there's a strong clue that the sages were talking about corporal punishment. They used the Hebrew word *sebet*: rod. That was a stick shepherds carried.

Most scholars agree the sages weren't using "rod" symbolically any more than an upset father would be thinking metaphorically when he orders his son to go get "the belt." People in Bible times spanked their kids. Historians say it was common throughout the ancient Middle East.

Clearly, most scholars insist, the sages of Proverbs recommended spanking. But did they order it? And even if they did, would God have signed off on beating kids?

Most scholars say the sages did not order parents to spank their kids. The sages simply ordered parents to discipline their kids—and spank them if necessary.

Spank does not mean clobber with a club, some scholars warn. Shepherds don't generally use rods that way—at least not on the sheep entrusted to their care. Instead, shepherds use the rods to protect their sheep—to gently nudge them back to the flock when they're in danger of nibbling their way into trouble.

When sages offer their advice on parenting, are they speaking for God?

Not necessarily, many Christians argue. Proverbs, most scholars agree, is a collection of wise sayings from elderly men to young men. These sayings are often general observations the sages have made after a lifetime of living. They're not necessarily promises or orders from God.

For example, it might be generally true that "lazy hands bring poverty, but hard-working hands bring riches" (Proverbs 10:4). Yet try selling that one-liner to a single mom working two jobs to keep food on the table and debt collectors off the front porch.

The sages weren't offering God's guarantee that spanking cures a child of foolishness, and will "remove it far from him" (Proverbs 22:15). For some kids there is no cure, short of learning their lessons the hard way.

The question for Christian parents today is whether or not the ancient practice of spanking is still necessary, given the many options now available. As in, "Get your homework done or I'll put your cell phone in time-out."

Some sensitive kids don't need much more than a stern look or a sharp tone of voice. One glaring eye from Mom or Dad, and they shape up.

Yet many Christians insist there are times when kids need to feel the sting of a swat—and that spanking is the wise thing to do, as the sages suggest.

Other Christians would quote the same sages to warn that if there's spanking to do, it shouldn't be done in a flare-up of anger: "It's smart to be patient, but it's stupid to lose your temper" (Proverbs 14:29 CEV).

72 Why do Christians say the prophet Isaiah predicted the virgin birth of Jesus 700 years ahead of time? Bible experts say that Isaiah was talking about a child born during his own time—and that "virgin" is a translation mistake.

Many Bible experts say that some of Isaiah's prophecies—this one included—pulled a double shift.

First shift: Isaiah's day.

Second shift: Jesus' day.

Others say Matthew took Isaiah's prophecy out of context to make it fit the Jesus story—like a preacher tweaking the facts of an illustration to make it better fit the sermon.

Matthew, more than any other gospel writer, quoted Old Testament prophecies to show that Jesus fulfilled them. Matthew did this to help prove that Jesus was the Messiah. Matthew quoted fifty-seven prophecies. Mark, the distant runner-up, quoted only about half as many: thirty.

When Isaiah spoke the prophecy, he intended it as a sign for his king, Ahaz, in the southern Jewish nation of Judah. Ahaz was getting bullied by two neighboring nations: the northern Jewish nation of Israel, along with Syria. Those two nations wanted Judah to join their coalition army to fight off the Assyrians—invaders from what is now Iraq. When Ahaz refused to join the coalition, the two neighboring nations turned on him and planned to replace him with a more cooperative king.

Isaiah's prophecy was crafted to assure the king that he had nothing to worry about. Isaiah told him that God would destroy both nations:

> The young woman is with child and shall bear a son, and shall name him Immanuel. . . . Before the child knows how to refuse the evil and choose the good, the land before whose two kings you are in dread will be deserted.
>
> Isaiah 7:14, 16 NRSV

Who is the "young woman" Isaiah was talking about? Guesses include a woman the king was engaged to marry or maybe even Isaiah's wife.

The writer used an odd Hebrew word to describe this mystery woman. Not *issah* (woman). Not *na'arah* (girl). He used *almah*. This word usually refers to a young woman of marrying age. That would make her a virgin if she's not married and sexually kosher.

That may be why Jews translating their Bible into Greek, about 100 years before Jesus, used the word *parthenos* to describe the woman. It means "virgin."

That translation is likely the version Matthew read, since he wrote his gospel in Greek, the international language of the day. When Matthew read that ancient prophecy in Greek, he apparently saw in it part of the story of Jesus.

• Mary, the virgin

• Jesus, Immanuel (God with us)

So Matthew tells Mary's story and then links it to Isaiah's prophecy: "All this happened so that what the Lord had spoken through the prophet came true: 'The virgin will become pregnant and give birth to a son, and they will name him Immanuel,' which means 'God is with us'" (Matthew 1:22–23).

If Matthew got it right—and many Bible experts say he did—Isaiah himself may not have realized that his prophecy would get to work a second shift.

73 Jacob had an all-night wrestling match with an angel? That's got to be a metaphor, right?

Maybe. Maybe not.

Many Bible experts say the mystery man that Jacob wrestled all night was probably a manifestation of God. (See Question 14, "Inconsistency alert: 'No one has ever seen God'. . .")

As the story goes, Jacob had left what is now Turkey and was headed back to his homeland in what is now Israel. He fled twenty years earlier, after his brother Esau vowed to kill him for cheating him out of his father's blessing.

On the night before crossing the Jordan River and reuniting with Esau, a worried Jacob withdrew from the caravan to spend some time alone.

That's where the story gets weird:

A man wrestled with him until dawn. When the man saw that he could not win against Jacob, he touched the socket of Jacob's hip so that it was dislocated as they wrestled. Then the man said, "Let me go; it's almost dawn."

Genesis 32:24–26

Okay, if that mystery man was God, this story begs a couple of questions.

Why would any high school wrestler going into a championship match pray for the help of a God who couldn't outwrestle a ninety-seven-year-old goat herder?

And what wrestling hold did Jacob use to tie up God all night—the step-over armlock camel clutch?

Most Bible scholars don't admit it—at least not in writing—but they're baffled by this story. That much seems obvious, because though they typically comment on the details in the story, they don't offer any compelling explanation about what in the dickens was going on.

They might as well describe in detail an elephant, and skip the part about why it's standing upside down on the ceiling. The elephant in this particular room: God dropping out of heaven to wrestle Jacob.

Some scholars have speculated that this bizarre scene is the patchwork of stories based on a legend about Jacob encountering a Canaanite god of the river ford. There are ancient Middle Eastern stories about gods or their servants guarding gateways, such as entrances into cities or palaces. A sandbar-like ford across a river was sometimes considered a bridge or gateway into a land.

Most Christians have trouble warming up to a theory like that—a theory suggesting the story is a myth. They prefer to read the report as a fact of history, and then file their unanswered questions under "Pending."

Whether the story is fact or fiction, many scholars say they see a lot of symbolism in it.

Wrestling tie-up. There's something spiritual going on here, some say. Though the wrestlers are locked in what sounds like a tie-up, it seems that the mystery man could easily break free. With a mere touch, he dislocated Jacob's hip. Some scholars say that what the mystery man couldn't overcome had nothing to do with physics. It was something spiritual. Jacob, in some way, was resisting God.

Demanding a blessing. Jacob was asking for God's help in what he was about to face. Scholars say this story would have made more sense to readers in ancient times. That's because there are other ancient Middle Eastern stories about gods held hostage for a reward. In one story, Jupiter, the Roman king of gods, asks a woman clutching him, "Why do you hold me? It is time. I want to get out of the city before daybreak" (*Amphitryon*). Then Jupiter gives the woman—with whom he has had sex—a golden bowl.

New name: Israel. Jacob gets renamed *Israel*. That's a good thing, since his original name sounds like the Hebrew word for "heel." He got that name because he was born clutching the heel of his twin brother, Esau. Jacob's new name—which the Jews would later adopt as the name of their nation—reflected his new character and his bright future: "Your name will no longer be Jacob but Israel [He Struggles With God], because you have struggled with God and with men—and you have won" (Genesis 32:28).

Dawn. This symbolized a new day for Jacob, some scholars say. He submitted himself to God and became a new man. From this point on in his story, he's no longer the heel we've read about in the earlier stories.

74 If God's so compassionate and wise, why did he condone slavery?

S lavery was a job in Bible times.

And an excellent argument for unions, some might add.

Today, we can make a solid case against slavery—arguing effectively that it's wrong for so many reasons. But if we had to haul our evidence into court, we probably wouldn't be offering the Bible as Exhibit A. Or Z. We might not mention the Bible at all.

Though the Bible talks a lot about slavery and in some places regulates it with laws, the Bible doesn't condemn it. Not once.

There were mainly two kinds of slaves in Bible times.

Willing slaves. Some agreed to become a slave for a set time to pay off a debt or to earn money.

Instead of working for The Man forty hours a week, these slaves hired themselves out 24/7, often for years: "If one of your own people sells himself to you as a slave, whether it is a Hebrew man or woman, that person will serve you for six years. But in the seventh year you must let the slave go free" (Deuteronomy 15:12 NCV).

Unwilling slaves. Most slaves in New Testament times were captives.

Soldiers or raiders captured them during an attack on a community. Pirates took them, along with everything else on the ships they boarded. Governments turned on an entire race of its citizens or guests—which is how the Jews ended up enslaved in Egypt until Moses came along.

Many Christians today are disappointed that the Bible writers failed to speak out against slavery. Even ashamed, perhaps. As ashamed as they are of Christians who owned slaves a couple of hundred years ago, and used Bible verses like these to defend the practice:

Slaves, obey your earthly masters with proper respect. Be as sincere as you are when you obey Christ. Don't obey them only while you're being watched, as if you merely wanted to please people. But obey like slaves who belong to Christ, who have a deep desire to do what God wants them to do. Serve eagerly as if you were serving your heavenly master and not merely serving human masters. You know that your heavenly master will reward all of us for whatever good we do, whether we're slaves or free people.

Ephesians 6:5–8

What was the apostle Paul thinking when he wrote those words to the church in Ephesus, on the west coast of what is now Turkey? And why on earth did he send the runaway slave, Onesimus, back to his master, Philemon? And while we're on the topic, why was Philemon—a Christian, and the host to a congregation that worshiped in his home—a slave owner?

Bible commentators generally respond with two points. They say we should keep both of them in mind while passing judgment on God's people from our distance of 2,000 years or more.

Times were different. Slavery was widely accepted and practiced. Changing that would not be quick and easy. In the meantime, the Jewish Bible regulated slavery in an attempt to protect slaves from abuse:

- If a woman sold into slavery didn't please her master, "he must let her be bought back by one of her close relatives" (Exodus 21:8).
- "In this jubilee year [every fifty years] every slave will be freed in order to return to his property" (Leviticus 25:13).

Paul got the ball rolling. Paul was no fan of slavery. But scholars speculate that he didn't want leaders of the Roman Empire to see the emerging Christian movement as a threat to the Roman way of life.

The empire was overrun with slaves. The Roman senate rejected the idea of dressing slaves in uniforms because it would allow the slaves to see how many there were of them—more than enough to threaten the empire in a revolt.

Though Paul didn't come right out and criticize slavery, he certainly planted seeds that would sprout in the hearts of Christian slave owners and eventually change their attitudes.

- "There are neither Jews nor Greeks, slaves nor free people, males nor females. You are all the same in Christ Jesus" (Galatians 3:28).
- "He [runaway slave Onesimus] is no longer like a slave to you. He is more than a slave, for he is a beloved brother, especially to me. Now he will mean much more to you, both as a man and as a brother in the Lord" (Philemon 1:16 NLT).
- "Masters, treat your slaves with respect. Don't threaten a slave. You know that there is one master in heaven who has authority over both of you, and he doesn't play favorites" (Ephesians 6:9).

Paul must have figured that, in the long haul, it would be impossible for a Christian slave owner to treat slaves with respect and brotherly love while at the same time robbing them of their freedom. Some scholars would say Paul was probably counting on it.

 75 Who should we believe about grounds for divorce? Moses, Jesus, or Paul? They each gave different advice.

Churches can't agree on what to do with divorced people, especially those who get remarried.

- Treat them as adulterers and refuse to let them take Communion: Roman Catholic.

- Reject them as pastors: many Baptist churches.
- Accept them with full privileges: many Methodist churches.

The reason churches treat divorced and remarried people so differently, some scholars explain, is because of the Bible. They say it sends mixed messages.

Quick and easy divorce

Moses: "If a man marries a woman and then it happens that he no longer likes her because he has found something wrong with her, he may give her divorce papers, put them in her hand, and send her off" (Deuteronomy 24:1 THE MESSAGE).

Adultery-only divorce

Jesus: "Anyone who divorces his wife, except for sexual immorality, makes her the victim of adultery, and anyone who marries a divorced woman commits adultery" (Matthew 5:32 NIV).

Abandonment divorce

Paul: "If the unbelieving partners leave, let them go. Under these circumstances a Christian man or Christian woman is not bound by a marriage vow. God has called you to live in peace" (1 Corinthians 7:15).

The quote attributed to Jesus is the biggest problem. It sounds like something a bachelor might say—someone ignorant of what else could go wrong with a marriage, other than adultery.

To name a few:

- The flip side of adultery: a husband with the romantic sense of an oxcart or a wife with the sex drive of a mud brick.

- Anger management problems: a partner who makes you feel like you're walking in a field of land mines, never knowing when things are going to blow.
- Addicted to bad stuff: a partner who can't seem to stop getting drunk, getting high, or getting the paycheck to disappear into shopping carts or gambling debts.

Some scholars trying to interpret Jesus' single ground for divorce often say he was using exaggeration in his debate with the Jews over what Moses said, trying to define what "something wrong" meant.

Followers of Rabbi Shammai (about 50 BC–AD 30) argued that Moses was talking about something terribly wrong, such as adultery.

But the majority of Jews, followers of Rabbi Hillel (about 70 BC–AD 10), said Moses was including anything the husband might consider displeasing:

- talking with a stranger
- letting herself go, until she starts to look like her brother
- failing to heal quickly from a dog bite.

Rough—if you were a woman.

Many scholars say Jesus, with hyperbole, pointed people away from the quick and easy divorce.

He explained why Moses allowed men to divorce their wives with nothing more than a written note (Mark 10:4).

He said, "He wrote this command for you because you're heartless" (v. 5). Did Jesus mean Moses allowed for divorce so heartless men wouldn't do even more terrible things to their wives? If so, many argue, Jesus probably didn't intend to make adultery the only ground for divorce.

And even then, adultery didn't need to kill a marriage. When Jesus forgave an adulteress instead of punishing her, some say he set a graceful example for husbands and wives struggling over what to do about an unfaithful spouse. Forgiveness is an option.

For many scholars, Paul's quote is the clincher.

They say it shows that as far as the Bible is concerned, adultery isn't the only legit ground for divorce. So is abandonment.

If we take to heart Paul's closing sentence on the matter—"God has called you to live in peace"—we can easily come up with other chronic marital problems that can evaporate peace into a dark cloud. More grounds for divorce?

Perhaps, many say, divorce should remain an option of last resort. If for no other reason, because of this one-liner from God: "I hate divorce" (Malachi 2:16).

76 The Old Testament penalty for raping a virgin: the rapist had to marry his victim. How is that not twisted?

If ever anyone doubted it was a man's world in Bible times, here's the cure:

> This is what you must do when a man rapes a virgin who isn't engaged. When the crime is discovered, the man who had sexual intercourse with her must give the girl's father 1¼ pounds [570 grams] of silver, and she will become his wife. Since he raped her, he can never divorce her as long as he lives.
>
> Deuteronomy 22:28–29

The rape victim had to marry her rapist.
She could never get a divorce.

Had she been married or even engaged, the rapist "must die" (Deuteronomy 22:23–24), not because he raped the woman, but because he violated another man's wife.

It was all about men: alpha dogs in the family and society.

Some scholars say the father of the raped woman had the option of taking the money and rejecting the marriage. An earlier version of what sounds like the same law adds: "But if her father refuses to let him marry her, the man must still pay him an amount equal to the bride price of a virgin" (Exodus 22:17 NLT).

Why would any father want to marry off his daughter to her rapist? And why would any woman in her right mind want to marry a man who had raped her and stolen her virginity?

There might be a hint of an answer in the story of what happened to one of King David's daughters after her half-brother, Amnon, raped her.

The princess was Tamar. She lived with David's other daughters in palace accommodations for royal virgins.

After her rape, she moved out: "Tamar lived as a desolate woman in her brother Absalom's house" (2 Samuel 13:20). There's no indication she ever married.

Even a defiled princess was considered damaged goods.

Women were property, bought and paid for. Most men didn't want to buy an inferior product—at least not when it came to a wife who would play such an important role in the survival of the family.

Scholars explain that this Jewish law, which sounds so harsh to us today, offered at least some security for women no one else would want. Women like this could count on having a husband till death they do part—which is more than other Jewish women could count on. (See Question 75, "Who should we believe about grounds for divorce? . . .")

Did God have anything to do with writing this law?

Many Christians, probably most, say they believe that the Bible got it right when it quoted Moses attributing the laws to God: "These are the commands, laws, and rules that the Lord your God commanded me to teach you" (Deuteronomy 6:1).

Some Christians, however, say they wonder if some of the ancient laws we're reading today in our "copies of copies" of the Bible are not always close to the originals.

Many scholars say Jews didn't compile these laws until several centuries after Moses, who lived in either the 1400s or the 1200s BC (scholars debate which). Some say the book of Deuteronomy was the work of one or more historians during the Jewish exile (500s BC) in what is now Iraq. They say that the writing styles suggest the historians drew from several sources.

Ancient Jewish tradition says Moses wrote the book, which has been carefully preserved. Many Christians seem to lean in that direction, or at least in the direction that Moses provided the reliable source material for the editors who compiled the final edition of Deuteronomy.

77 Why did Ezra order Jewish men who married non-Jews to divorce their wives and send them and their kids away? Not kind.

In all fairness, there's no indication God signed off on what many say sounds like a crazy idea:

> Some Israelite men have married foreign women. . . . And now God's holy people are mixed with foreigners. . . . We must promise God that we will divorce our foreign wives and send them away, together with their children.
>
> Ezra 9:2; 10:3 CEV

Many Jewish men actually did this in the 400s BC after returning to Israel from exile in what is now Iraq.

Family, be gone.

What's odd about it is that Israel's greatest dynasty of kings had come from a mixed marriage. King David's great-grandmother Ruth was not a Jew. She came from what is now the Arab country of Jordan. Widowed there, Ruth moved to Bethlehem with her mother-in-law, Naomi, and then married Boaz, a Jewish farmer.

Some scholars say Ruth's wonderfully crafted story was added to the Bible's library of books as a counterpoint to Ezra's callous command.

In fairness to Ezra, many scholars say there was reason for the Jews to worry. They had lost their nation—wiped completely off the political map—because they had married outside the Jewish faith and then they adopted the idol-worshiping religions of their spouses.

Prophets told them that sins like these, especially worshiping idols, were the reason God let invaders drive them out of their homeland in 586 BC.

The sin started with David's son: "King Solomon loved many foreign women. . . . In his old age, his wives tempted him to follow other gods. He was no longer committed to the Lord his God as his father David had been" (1 Kings 11:1, 4).

Now, 600 years later, Ezra and his fellow Jews had returned to Israel to rebuild their nation from ashes. But already it looked like the Jews had jumped back on the sin cycle.

So said a mysterious man named "Shecaniah, son of Jehiel" (Ezra 10:2). He's the one who asked Ezra to order the mass divorce.

Some scholars say they suspect Shecaniah's motives because his father is listed among the 113 Jewish men married to non-Jews: "From the descendants of Elam . . . Jehiel" (Ezra 10:26).

Let's say Jehiel had two wives: one Jewish and another non-Jewish. Obviously, Shecaniah would have been born to the Jewish mother. If Shecaniah managed to get his brothers from the non-Jewish wife sent away, he would have inherited a bigger chunk of the family estate. Maybe all of it.

Whatever Shecaniah's motive for making the request, Ezra and the other Jewish leaders bought in to it.

If Jewish leaders had issued that decree some 600 years earlier, Boaz would have divorced Ruth and sent her away with her son, King David's grandpa.

78 Jesus said, "If your eye—even your good eye— causes you to lust, gouge it out and throw it away." Wouldn't that leave just about everyone with a couple of extra holes in their head?

The literal translation of Matthew 5:29 (NLT) invites us to poke out our right eye. We could still watch television, but we'd probably not pay extra for the 3-D channels.

Poking out our eye isn't what Jesus was suggesting, Bible commentators agree. Jesus, using exaggeration, was making pretty much the same point that one particular children's song makes: "Oh, be careful little eyes what you see."

Here's the context: Jesus was talking about adultery. That sin is a big deal—prohibited by commandment number seven of the famous ten: "Never commit adultery" (Exodus 20:14).

As far as Jesus was concerned, adultery starts long before anyone gets naked: "I can guarantee that whoever looks with lust at a woman has already committed adultery in his heart" (Matthew 5:28).

This is the spot in Jesus' sermon where he suggested popping out the right eye. He may have picked the right eye, scholars say, because folks considered the right eye, like the right hand, the dominant one.

Jesus' point: adultery begins in the eyes.

Remember the very married King David and his dalliance with Bathsheba, who was married to one of David's elite strike force warriors? David, walking on his palace roof one afternoon, saw Bathsheba taking a bath below. She may have been in the walled courtyard of her home, or inside by a window. Wherever, David had the angle.

David not only saw her, he kept looking.

The Message version of the Bible translates Jesus' advice this way, which could have been helpful to David: "If you want to live a morally pure life, here's what you have to do: You have to blind your right eye the moment you catch it in a lustful leer" (v. 29).

It's not the eyeballs Jesus wants us to get rid of, scholars say. It's the temptation that the eyes see. The eyes can lead us to follow our nose into danger zones. One of many danger zones for a husband is someone else's wife—or any other woman who catches his eye.

Elderly Job seemed to practice what Jesus preached: "I made an agreement with my eyes. I promised not to look at another woman with sexual longing" (Job 31:1 NIRV).

 79 Jesus said, "Be perfect, just as your Father in heaven is perfect" (Matthew 5:48). Isn't that just a little too much to expect from anything short of a celestial being?

Taken as a sound bite, "be perfect" feels like a stretch—fit for souls made of elastic, not flesh.

We're only human.

We're going to think bad thoughts every day.

We're going to get into trouble sometime after we slap our feet onto the floor.

We're going to say something stupid at least once a day—more often if we're a preacher or a politician.

But none of that has anything to do with what Jesus was talking about. "Be perfect" is how Jesus summed up a paragraph about loving not only our neighbors but our enemies as well. Jesus doesn't expect us to be perfect in everything we do. He's not a soccer mom.

He wants us to work on perfecting our love for other people. Most Bible scholars seem to agree on that interpretation. That's because Jesus seems to start this love topic by giving a few specific examples before summing up the principle behind those examples:

- If someone slaps you, turn the other cheek.
- If someone wants your coat, give them your shirt, too.
- If someone asks you to carry something for a mile, go the extra mile.
- Pray for your enemies.

"In this way you show that you are children of your Father in heaven" (Matthew 5:45).

When we love others the way God loves us, we love others just the way they are. That doesn't mean we're okay with the way they are. We may be very not okay with the way they are. Certainly, God's not okay with us when we hurt ourselves or others. But he loves us anyhow.

And he's always near, the Bible says, ready to help: "The Lord will watch over your life no matter where you go, both now and forever" (Psalm 121:8 NIRV).

Perfect love is like that.

This brand of love was a life goal for the apostle Paul: "I have not yet reached my goal, and I am not perfect. But Christ has taken hold of me. So I keep on running and struggling to take hold of the prize. . . . I run toward the goal, so that I can win the prize of being called to heaven. This is the prize that God offers because of what Christ Jesus has done" (Philippians 3:12, 14 CEV).

Perfect love is a goal that Christians chase.

80 King David wrote, "I have never seen the godly abandoned or their children begging for bread." Was that wishful thinking, a promise from God, or a clue that David needed to get out of the palace a little more often?

David knew better. He begged for bread—twice.

- **Once from a priest:** "Give me five loaves of bread or whatever you can find" (1 Samuel 21:3).
- **Once from a shepherd, Nabal, who refused:** "Should I take my bread, my water, and my meat that I butchered for my shearers and give them to men coming from who knows where?" (1 Samuel 25:11).

Actually, scholars say they're not certain David wrote the song about never having seen the godly abandoned. It's attributed to him in a vague way, as a song "of David." Scholars say it may have been by him, about him, or dedicated to him.

Scholars also defend the writer's statement, preserved in Psalm 37:25 (NLT). They call it a generalization and compare it to a proverb that uses exaggeration to encourage people. The Bible experts say the writer knew there were exceptions to the rule—temporary times when it feels as though God has abandoned us.

In fact, they say the writer may have had those very people in mind when he wrote this song, intending to remind desperate souls in tough situations that God is still looking out for them.

Over the long haul of life—the writer describes himself as "old"—God doesn't abandon his people. That's the message of the song, scholars say. God is there with us, even during times of loneliness, hunger, and suffering.

 81 Where did religious people get the idea they would live forever? The Bible says, "The dead cannot sing praises to the Lord, for they have gone into the silence of the grave."

It seems true enough, if the Jewish Bible is any clue: Most Jews before the time of Jesus seemed to believe that dead was dead. Period.

These early Jews might well have agreed with one popular epitaph scratched into Roman gravestones throughout the empire: "I was not. I was. I am not. I care not." From nothing, to life, to nothing again.

In addition to Psalm 115:17 (NLT), quoted in the question above, here are some other clues that many Jews believed this:

- "Lord, . . . dead people don't remember you; those in the grave don't praise you" (Psalm 6:4–5 NCV).
- "You are God from everlasting to everlasting. You turn mortals back into dust" (Psalm 90:2–3).
- "They will fall into a deep sleep and never wake up" (Jeremiah 51:57).

Yet some Jews seemed to believe in a mysterious place of the dead. In one story, the prophet Samuel came back from the dead long enough to give King Saul some rotten news on the night before he led Israel into battle with the Philistines: "Tomorrow you and your sons will be with me" (1 Samuel 28:19).

Bible experts who work on putting dates to when Bible books were written—based on writing styles and content clues—say the first clear Bible reference to an afterlife doesn't show up until about 175 years before Jesus.

It comes in a prophecy in the book of Daniel, which many Bible experts say was edited together long after the prophet Daniel, who lived in the 500s BC: "Many people who have already died will live again. Some of them will wake up to have life forever, but some will wake up to find shame and disgrace forever" (Daniel 12:2 NCV).

Many Bible historians speculate that Jews picked up ideas about an afterlife from Persians, during the Jewish exile (500s–400s BC) in what is now Iraq and Iran. Other Bible scholars say it was more of a God thing—a gradual revelation to the people.

By the time of Jesus, Jews were divided on the matter. One first-century Jewish historian, Josephus (about AD 37–101), said the Jewish group called Pharisees believed in "an immortal soul."

Another branch of the Jewish faith, the Sadducees, didn't believe in an afterlife—which some seminary profs tell their students is why Sadducees were "sad you see." It's a cheesy memory trick to help students remember that fact about the group. But it works.

Wherever Jews got the idea of an afterlife, Jesus confirmed it when he told the Sadducees they got it wrong:

When the dead come back to life, . . . they are like the angels in heaven. Haven't you read in the book of Moses that the dead come back to life? It's in the passage about the bush, where God said, "I am the God of Abraham, Isaac, and Jacob." He's not the God of the dead but of the living. You're badly mistaken!

Mark 12:25–27

Jesus' point was that if Abraham, Isaac, and Jacob—who had lived several centuries before Moses—were dead as doornails, God would have said, "I WAS the God of Abraham, Isaac, and Jacob." Past tense.

But God is not the great I Was. He assured Moses that he's the great "I Am" (Exodus 3:14).

New Testament writers didn't describe eternal life as something out there in the future. Quoting Jesus, they said it begins in this life when people put their trust in God: "I tell you the truth, whoever hears what I say and believes in the One who sent me has eternal life. That person will not be judged guilty but has already left death and entered life" (John 5:24 NCV).

82 Inconsistency alert: Jews sang a song blessing anyone who would smash their enemies' babies against the rocks. How does that track with Jesus' "love your enemies"?

Let's say a foreign country invaded, overran, and conquered the United States. They killed most Americans. To kill babies, they saved their ammo. They grabbed the babies by the ankles and smashed their heads onto the concrete.

They bombed Washington DC and most other major cities into the Stone Age. Then they deported American survivors to refugee camps in their homeland. And then they asked the Grammy-winning musicians among the refugees to entertain everyone with American music—"The Star-Spangled Banner" to begin with.

If we said our prayers that first night in the refugee camp, what would we pray?

Psalm 137 is that kind of prayer, many scholars would agree.

It's a lament. It's an angry, gut-twisting, teeth-grinding demand for payback—an eye for an eye, a tooth for a tooth, and a smashed baby skull for a smashed baby skull.

Babylonian invaders from what is now Iraq had wiped the Jewish nation off the political map. They leveled Jerusalem and other major cities. They bashed in the heads of Jewish babies. They deported Jewish survivors to Babylon. And then they had the audacity to ask the refugees to "Sing a song from Zion for us!" (Psalm 137:3).

Zion was Jerusalem, a holy city the Babylonians had leveled—destroying the world's only Jewish temple.

The book of Psalms is a collection of Jewish songs and prayers that cover just about every emotion people feel when they talk to God. Sometimes when we talk to God, we're thankful—and we tell him so. But sometimes we're confused, worried, mad at the world, or mad at God—and we tell him so.

Psalm 137 is a song sung blue. It's not a theology we're to study and apply to our lives. Scholars agree on that.

The prayer comes from a poignant moment in the life of someone who had lost almost everything. This is someone we're to empathize with—to recognize the brokenness and the need for a degree of healing that only God could provide.

This cry of pain is the person's first call to God.

83 Where do Christians get the idea that an evil antichrist is coming to rule the world? When the Bible writer mentions an antichrist, he's talking about people in his own day who don't buy into the Jesus story.

Christians pieced the antichrist together like a Frankenstein, some Bible scholars say—though most wouldn't put it quite that graphically.

As church historians explain the process, sometime during the Middle Ages—between AD 600 and 1000, before the infamous Crusades—preachers began stealing body parts from evil characters throughout the New Testament and stitching them together to make one nasty enemy of everything good.

That made for some hair-raising preaching.

The preachers started with the antichrist mentioned briefly in only four passages pulled from the tiny letters of John.

Here is everything the Bible says about the antichrist—who turns out to be a no-show in the end-time book of Revelation:

- **He's already here, and he brought company.** "You heard that Antichrist is coming. Well, they're all over the place, antichrists everywhere you look" (1 John 2:18 THE MESSAGE).
- **How to spot an antichrist, part 1.** "This is what makes an antichrist: denying the Father, denying the Son" (1 John 2:22 THE MESSAGE).
- **How to spot an antichrist, part 2.** "Every person who doesn't declare that Jesus Christ has come as a human has a spirit that isn't from God. This is the spirit of the antichrist that you have heard is coming. That spirit is already in the world" (1 John 4:2–3).

- **Antichrists say Jesus wasn't flesh and blood.** "There are a lot of smooth-talking charlatans loose in the world who refuse to believe that Jesus Christ was truly human, a flesh-and-blood human being. Give them their true title: Deceiver! Antichrist!" (2 John 1:7 THE MESSAGE).

When John talked about folks believing Jesus wasn't human, scholars say he may have been pointing to an early heresy. Some Christians in the first few centuries taught that Jesus wasn't human, but that he was merely a spirit who pretended to be human—and pretended to die and rise from the dead.

Probably beginning in the Middle Ages, historians speculate, preachers started connecting some disconnected bad guys in the Bible, forming a composite character—an enemy of God and everything he stands for.

Antichrist: "You've heard that an antichrist is coming" (1 John 2:18).

Man of lawlessness: "Let us clarify some things about the coming of our Lord Jesus Christ. . . . That day will not come until there is a great rebellion against God and the man of lawlessness is revealed—the one who brings destruction. He will exalt himself and defy everything that people call god and every object of worship. He will even sit in the temple of God, claiming that he himself is God" (2 Thessalonians 2:1, 3–4 NLT).

Beast: "The beast was given a mouth to brag and speak evil things against God. . . . He was allowed to make war against God's people and to overcome them. He was given authority over every tribe, people, language and nation" (Revelation 13:5, 7 NIRV).

Many Bible scholars today argue that the Beast and the man of lawlessness sound a lot like the Roman Empire. Roman general Titus went inside the last Jewish temple of God shortly before his men leveled it.

Other scholars say the descriptions might pull double duty, referring both to Roman times and to a time yet to come. Some

Bible prophecies do seem to work that way, many scholars say. (See Question 72, about Isaiah's prophecy of a virgin birth.)

84 Paul agreed with a poet who said, "The people of Crete are all liars, cruel animals, and lazy gluttons." That probably didn't endear him to the people of Crete, right?

Paul wasn't the most delicate writer in the Bible. He could be blunt.

He once royally told off some Jewish Christians who kept nagging Gentile Christians to follow the Jewish laws and get circumcised. In perhaps his harshest rebuke in all of his Bible writings, he said, "Why don't these agitators, obsessive as they are about circumcision, go all the way and castrate themselves!" (Galatians 5:12 THE MESSAGE).

Ouch.

Dealing with people as blunt as Paul can be unsettling. But at least we always know exactly what they think and where we stand with them.

In fairness to Paul, this quote about the people of Crete (Titus 1:12–13) originally came from a native of Crete: Epimenides (about 600s BC). Writing in a poem called *Cretica*, Epimenides had Minos the king of Crete telling the god Zeus: "Cretans, always liars, evil beasts, idle bellies."

So when Paul said he agreed, he was agreeing with a Cretan poet quoting a Cretan king.

In time, the Greek word for Cretan—*Kretizo*—became a verb: "to lie."

Even so, many would argue that it's one thing for Cretans to say that about themselves—self-deprecation is allowed. It's quite another thing for someone else to say that—belittling isn't kosher.

Though Paul's quote ended up in the Bible, it began as a passing thought in a personal letter he wrote to Titus, a minister he had assigned to plant churches on the island of Crete. Had Paul known his letter would end up in the Bible, forever offending Cretans, some students of the Bible say he might have tweaked a few words.

Essentially, Paul was saying that Titus had what might seem like a mission impossible. On this island with a scumbag reputation, Titus had to find a few good men—to lead churches in cities throughout Crete: "I left you in Crete to do what still needed to be done—appointing spiritual leaders in every city as I directed you. A spiritual leader must have a good reputation" (Titus 1:5–6).

Titus apparently found some. Today, most of the half-million Cretans who live there are members of the Greek Orthodox Church.

85 Jesus said that everyone who follows him must hate their family. Why would anyone follow him?

Jesus sometimes used shock and awe to get the attention of the crowd—exaggeration.

Most scholars say that's what he was doing in Luke 14:26. Jesus didn't literally want us to hate our families. He defended families.

Once Jesus criticized religious leaders for encouraging people to put their religious practices above the needs of their families: "You say it is all right for people to say to their parents, 'Sorry, I can't help you. For I have vowed to give to God what I would have given to you.' In this way, you let them disregard their needy parents" (Mark 7:11–12 NLT).

In other words, many students of the Bible conclude, Jesus was saying we need to make sure our parents are taken care of before we take care of the worship center. We don't give our last spare thousand dollars to the church's building fund when our parents are in desperate need of a thousand dollars to cover the rent or to buy food and medicine.

On the other hand, there are times when our families can get in the way of our faith—just as building our own kingdoms of wealth can become more important to us than building God's kingdom.

Some would argue that a key point Jesus was trying to make is that we should not let our family prod us into doing something we know is wrong—or keep us from doing the right thing.

Let me give you a personal example. That's rare in books like this that I write. I normally stop at reporting what others say. But this comes from a recent experience.

I used to struggle over this passage because I could never imagine loving God so much that, by comparison, it would feel like I hated my family. I love my wife and my children more than I love my own life. I believe I would die to save any one of them.

Something happened a couple of weeks ago that changed the way I read this Bible passage. My daughter, Becca, and I were driving back home to the Kansas City area after visiting my mom, brothers, and sisters in Ohio. Becca is an RN who works in a hospital and is studying to become a nurse practitioner. We took the trip because she was on break from work and classes, and she wanted to take this last chance to visit the Ohio branch of our family before her wedding in a few months.

About fifty miles (80 km) east of St. Louis, westbound on I-70, we crested a hill to see a huge tractor-trailer crashed into the woods at the right side of the road.

It had just happened. The driver of the car traveling in front of us saw it all.

Becca was driving my car. She abruptly slowed down to dodge debris in the road.

Over at the crash site, I saw a body in the cab. It wasn't moving.

"Should we stop and help?" I asked Becca.

She didn't say a word, but she pulled the car to the side of the road.

As she stepped out on the traffic side of the expressway, I instantly became afraid for her. "Come over here and walk in the grass with me," I said. I was afraid a passing car might hit her—distracted drivers looking at the wreck.

We ran to the truck, which had plowed through a guardrail and mowed down trees thicker than my gut before wedging itself among the trees. The truck was ripped to pieces, the contents of its trailer scattered.

Two other drivers had already gotten to the scene. But they were just standing near the truck, doing nothing. I was afraid it was because there was nothing to do.

We discovered that two men were inside the cab. Both were in shock, paralyzed with confusion. The driver sat there, stunned. He was the motionless body I had seen. Another man, apparently the relief driver, must have been sleeping in the bed behind the driver. He was rummaging around, looking for a shoe.

My daughter and I stood at the foot of the cab, asking if the men were okay and urging them to get out right away.

I could see water pouring from the radiator. But what terrified me was catching a strong whiff of diesel fuel. While Becca focused on the men, I started looking for a leak.

I was afraid if the fuel came into contact with any hot metal on the engine, there could be an explosion—though I learned later that diesel doesn't usually explode. Yet as far as I was concerned at that moment, my daughter stood in the blast zone. I had put her in harm's way.

In the rush of those moments, it seemed like the Good Samaritan right thing to do. The godly thing to do. The "putting Jesus above self and family" thing to do.

We both did it automatically. I put her there. She put me there. Gladly, nothing exploded. The men survived with what looked like minor injuries.

The experience left me wondering if what happened on I-70 is one of the many expressions of faith that Jesus had in mind when he said everything and everyone must take second place to following him.

Disciples of Jesus do the right thing.

86 How could Daniel have possibly survived the night in a lion's den and three of his buddies survive getting tossed into a furnace?

Some Christians don't believe it.

They treat the stories as legends, inserted into a book written anonymously and compiled about 400 years after Daniel's lifetime.

The prophet Daniel and his three friends—Shadrach, Meshach, and Abednego—were taken captive from their Jewish homeland to what is now Iraq. Babylonian invaders took them and other uppercrust Jews in about 600 BC, and then later appointed them as royal advisors.

These Jews were intended as hostages to help keep the Jewish nation in line and under the thumb of the Babylonian Empire, superpower of the ancient Middle East.

Clues in Daniel's story and his prophecies—such as a slew of details that track dead-on with Greek Empire history in the centuries that followed—have led many Bible scholars to conclude that an editor or a team of editors compiled the book in the mid-100s

BC. That's when they say Daniel's predictions stop accurately re-flecting history. (See Question 34, "Daniel's prophecies about the Greek empire track nicely . . .")

Most Christians, however, seem to read the stories in Daniel as accurate history.

They argue that the fact that Daniel's predictions track so per-fectly with history simply proves he was the genuine article—a prophet of God.

Fiery furnace

As the fiery furnace story goes, Babylon's most famous king—Nebuchadnezzar—built a ninety-foot-tall (twenty-seven-meter) gold statue of himself. Ironically enough, he may have built it to commemorate a dream that Daniel had interpreted for him earlier. It was a dream about a huge statue: "The head of this statue was made of fine gold. Its chest and arms were made of silver. Its stomach and hips were made of bronze. Its legs were made of iron. Its feet were made partly of iron and partly of clay" (Daniel 2:32–33).

Daniel said the gold head represented Nebuchadnezzar's king-dom, which is superior to the kingdoms that would come later, and that were represented by the other, lesser materials.

Immediately after that story, the writer reports that Nebuchad-nezzar built the massive statue and ordered all his officials and advisors to bow down and worship it.

Daniel was apparently gone at the time. But his three colleagues weren't. They refused to worship the idol.

The king ordered them thrown into a "blazing furnace" (Dan-iel 3:20). It may have been a kiln used to harden bricks—perhaps the same kiln in which artisans made the statue. One ancient kiln uncovered in the area looks a bit like a railroad tunnel sealed at both ends. Workers would place the bricks on ledges inside, build a fire on the floor, and then seal the kiln, allowing just enough of an opening for air to fuel the fire.

Kilns like that could reach temperatures over 1,800 degrees Fahrenheit (982 Celsius). Cremation chambers today produce temps ranging from about 1,400–1,800 degrees Fahrenheit (760–982 Celsius).

As the story goes—a folktale according to some Christians—the king saw a fourth man standing with the three fireproof Jews: "The fourth one looks like a son of the gods" (Daniel 3:25). The king called the men out, "and they didn't smell of smoke" (Daniel 3:27).

Details like that, some Christians say, smack of the kind of exaggeration we would expect to find in a legend. So would the description that the king had ordered the fire stoked to "seven times hotter than normal" (Daniel 3:19).

Yet other Christians, probably most, argue that there's nothing in this story that God couldn't do.

The story ends with the king praising the Jewish God, promoting the three men, and ordering everyone in his empire to respect God since "no other god can rescue like this" (Daniel 3:29).

Lions' den

This story takes place years later, when the elderly Daniel was serving as the lead advisor for the king of the Persian Empire based in what is now Iran. Persians had conquered the Iraqi-based Babylonians and had taken control of the Middle East.

Jealous officials trying to get rid of Daniel manipulated the king into signing an irrevokable law ordering people to pray to no one but him for a month—or get fed to lions.

The officials knew the king's ego couldn't resist a law like that. And they knew Daniel's religion couldn't abide a law like that. He would keep praying to God. He did, and the officials had him arrested.

Once the king realized he had been manipulated into ordering the execution of his favorite advisor, he became angry. Yet he had no choice but to send Daniel to the lions.

The king spent a sleepless night worrying about Daniel. At first light, he rushed to the lions' den and called out for Daniel, who replied, "My God sent his angel and shut the lions' mouths so that they couldn't hurt me" (Daniel 6:22).

Relieved about Daniel and furious about being manipulated, the king served up his conniving officials as cat food.

The Bible says the king was Darius the Mede. He hasn't shown up in history. Scholars aren't sure what to do about that. Some say it's another clue this was a legend.

Cyrus was the king of Persia at the time, reigning from 559–530 BC. Perhaps, some scholars say, Darius was a general that Cyrus assigned to rule the conquered Babylonian homeland.

Others say *Darius* could have been a Babylonian name Cyrus adopted for the sake of Babylonian public relations. Cyrus was famous for treating conquered nations respectfully. He's the king who freed Jewish political prisoners to go home and rebuild Jerusalem and their homeland after Babylonians had leveled the cities (Ezra 1:1–4).

For some Christians, the story of Daniel in the lions' den is easier to swallow than the story of the fiery furnace. Lions not hungry? Possible. Fire that doesn't burn? Not in the world of physics.

87 Doesn't it seem a bit out of character for a holy God to tell a prophet to marry a hooker?

Jews and Christians have had a little trouble with this story. Their scholars throughout the centuries haven't liked it much. At least not as a literal read.

They knew God had asked other prophets to do fairly strange things, sometimes acting out their prophecies:

- **Jeremiah wasn't allowed to get married and have a family.** This was to drive home the point that Jewish families were about to die when Babylonians from what is now Iraq invaded (Jeremiah 16:1–4).
- **Ezekiel was told to tremble while eating.** It was to illustrate how the Jews would one day eat in fear while invaders decimated their homeland (Ezekiel 12:18–20).

Still, most Bible scholars couldn't bring themselves to believe that God would ask one of his prophets to go as far as Hosea did just to make a point: "Go and marry a prostitute, so that some of her children will be conceived in prostitution. This will illustrate how Israel has acted like a prostitute by turning against the Lord and worshiping other gods" (Hosea 1:2 NLT).

Really?

Ruin the rest of your life and the lives of the children that will be born, just to make a point you could convey in a sentence?

That doesn't sound godlike. Not as far as most scholars were concerned in centuries past.

Then and now, Bible experts offered up some speculation about this story.

One point to begin with: *prostitute* translates a word that could simply mean "loose woman"—as in, promiscuous. She may not have been a prostitute.

A few theories about the story:

Dream journal. Some Bible experts in the early centuries speculated that this story was actually a dream Hosea had. He woke up and told the story to the Jews to illustrate their spiritual prostitution. But there's no clue in the book that this was a dream—other than the "hard to believe" factor if it's not.

File under fiction, with parables. Not quite a parable, yet it's a cousin, some scholars guessed: allegory—a symbolic story. It might not have been a dream, but like a dream, it never really happened. That's the theory. Hosea dreamed it up in the daylight, with God's inspiration.

Good girl goes bad. Most Bible experts today say they don't buy either of those earlier theories. One alternate idea: read the story as a flashback. Hosea didn't marry a bad girl who gave him kids by other men in the neighborhood. He married a good girl who went bad later—like the nation of Israel did. Yet it seems unclear to some Christians how this theory paints God with brighter colors than the hard-core story, which has Hosea marrying a bad girl from the get-go. After all, God knew where she was going all along.

Bad to the bone. Most Bible experts today seem to rally behind the idea that the writer wants us to believe that Hosea's wife was bad all along. She started out bad, like the Jewish nation did— leaving a frustrated Moses to ask God, "Why don't you just kill me?" (Numbers 11:15). Hosea's wife, Gomer, ran off, apparently chasing other men—just as the Jews left God to chase after idols. Gomer ended up enslaved. So did the Jews.

Christians who read Hosea's story literally—either "good girl goes bad" or "bad to the bone"—will often admit that the story paints God with dark colors. But they would add that this was a dark time in Jewish history—perhaps the darkest of all. That's because the Jews were on the brink of losing just about everything.

Hosea ministered in the northern Jewish nation of Israel from about 750–722 BC. It seems he lived to see the lights go out in his nation. Assyrian invaders from what is now Iraq erased Israel from the political map in 722 BC. Assyrians deported the survivors and resettled the land with their own pioneers.

More than a century later, in 586 BC, Babylonian invaders erased the southern Jewish nation of Judah.

Israel was gone.

God brought them home fifty years later.

In Hosea's story, that's illustrated by God telling him to buy Gomer back.

In the same way, Hosea predicted, "Israel will turn back to the Lord their God" (Hosea 3:5 CEV).

88 Don't use God's name in vain—it's one of God's Ten Commandments. Isn't that a bit vain—as though it's more important than helping the poor, which didn't make the cut?

Some Bible experts say God wasn't protecting himself with the third commandment. He was protecting us from people who use his name to exploit and hurt us.

Take my pastor, for example.

He's nationally known, and our congregation is widely respected for helping the helpless here in our community and abroad.

Someone created a Facebook page that invoked my pastor's name, claiming to be him and his congregation. After people "liked" the fake page and exchanged posts, the fake pastor sent an invitation for his new friend to contribute to our church's mission effort in Africa—correctly naming the group we're currently helping. Fake Pastor gave a bank account number for making the transfer.

Real Pastor contacted the FBI.

Someone—likely in another country, given the broken English used—was trying to exploit others in the name of God and my pastor.

The fake pastor was breaking federal law as well as God's third commandment:

You shall not misuse the name of the Lord your God, for the Lord
will not hold anyone guiltless who misuses his name.

Exodus 20:7 NIV

Bible experts don't agree on exactly what it means to "misuse"
God's name.

Contenders: It's using God's name

- flippantly, jokingly, as in "Oh, my God!"
- cussing, as in "God dammit."
- swearing a dishonest oath, such as lying in court.

Many Jews refuse to even speak God's name, out of respect.

They'll use another word or phrase, such as *Hashem*, which is
Hebrew for "the name." Or they'll write his name: "G-d."

Even Matthew, writing the most Jewish-friendly of the four
Gospels, preferred the phrase "kingdom of heaven" over "kingdom
of God."

At its broadest, many scholars say, misusing God's name refers
to misrepresenting God.

One example that some Christians cite: prosperity preachers
who make a buck off God by selling the idea that people can strike
it rich by donating to their ministries: "'Bring to the storehouse
a full tenth of what you earn. . . . Test me in this,' says the Lord
All-Powerful. 'I will open the windows of heaven for you and pour
out all the blessings you need'" (Malachi 3:10 NCV).

As though God were talking to Christians about a TV ministry
instead of to Jews about their one and only worship center, the
Jerusalem temple.

Other ways that scholars say people hurt others in God's name:

- Making up rules they say are based on Bible principles—such
  as "Don't drink alcohol," and then telling people they have to
  obey these rules if they want to please God.

- Related to that, telling people they're going to hell if they don't interpret the Bible the way they're told to.
- Using Bible verses to attack people instead of help them.
- Launching violence and holy wars, such as the Crusades or jihad. Terrorists often die shouting, "God is great!"
- Behaving in an ungodly way, which makes God look bad. It reflects on him when people claim to be his children but act like the devil.

89 Inconsistency alert: Jesus said we should ask God not to lead us into temptation. But the Bible also says, "Do not say, 'God is tempting me.' . . . He never tempts anyone." Who's right?

Many scholars say Jesus (in Matthew 6:13) and James (in James 1:13 NLT)—who were brothers, according to ancient tradition—weren't talking about the same thing.

The Greek word that both of them used: *peirazo*, can run in two directions:

- **Temptation**—enticing someone to do something wrong.
- **Test**—an experience to prove someone's character or commitment.

Some scholars say Jesus was talking about testing: "Do not bring us to hard testing" (Matthew 6:13 GNT).

Others say Jesus was talking about temptation, but he wasn't suggesting God causes it: "Keep us from falling into sin when we are tempted" (NIRV).

None of the modern Bible translations of Matthew suggest God entices people to do anything evil.

But the Bible is full of examples of God's people up to their ears in tough situations that measure the depth of their faith.

Jesus said there would be days like that: "All nations will hate you because you are committed to me. Then many will lose faith" (Matthew 24:9–10).

That's a good description of what happened during the Roman persecution of Christians. Early Christian writings during the first three centuries report that almost all of Jesus' original dozen disciples died as martyrs.

90 Why do so many Christians get upset about drinking alcoholic beverages when the first reported miracle of Jesus was to turn enough water into wine to get over 1,000 people too drunk to drive a donkey cart?

Christians didn't seem to have a problem with drinking wine, beer, and other alcoholic beverages for about 1,800 years, church historians report.

John Wesley (1703–1791), British minister and founder of the Methodist Church, was one of the first big-name church leaders to come out against booze. He was okay with the mild drinks: wine and beer. But he shooed Christians away from hard liquor such as whiskey—which can woozy up a brain in just a few flicks of the wrist.

The Bible certainly condemns drunkenness (Romans 13:13; Ephesians 5:18).

But, according to church historians, the Bible isn't the reason so many Christians in the 1800s started jumping on the teetotaling bandwagon and roping reluctant stragglers to pull them on board, too.

As cities got bigger, more people seemed to get drunker.

A doctor named Benjamin Rush (1746–1813) lobbied against hard liquor, insisting it was addictive. Some preachers took his idea—and then some—to the pulpit. They began insisting that members of their congregation abstain from all alcohol.

Prohibition eventually followed in the United States, lasting thirteen unlucky years—as drinkers might describe the time (1920–1933). During that stretch, it was against the law to make and sell alcoholic drinks.

Today, Christians are divided when it comes to drinking.

Some churches still preach abstinence: many Baptist, Pentecostal, and some Methodist. Most, however, preach moderation: Catholic, Anglican, Lutheran, and Eastern Orthodox.

Many Bible experts agree that though people can make a case against drinking alcohol from a social and medical point of view— alcoholism, drunk driving, liver disease—there's no solid Bible argument for total abstinence.

Wine in the Bible wasn't grape juice.

Thomas Welch, a Methodist, invented grape juice in 1869. Before that, all grape juice turned into wine on its own because there was no refrigeration. The Welch company website says that Thomas and his son Charles developed the process of pasteurizing grape juice to provide non-fermented juice for churches to use for Communion.

In Israel, vintners harvested grapes in August and September, very hot months. The juice began to ferment the same day the grapes were pressed. It was ready to drink six weeks later, though folks preferred aged wine—as wine connoisseurs do today.

In his first miracle, Jesus made at least 120 gallons (454 liters) of wine—the good stuff, which the wedding planner praised: "You have saved the best wine for now" (John 2:10).

Three five-ounce glasses of wine—15 ounces (.44 liters)—can raise the blood alcohol content of an average-size person above .08 percent, making them legally intoxicated. There are 128 ounces (3.7 liters) in a gallon, so that means Jesus had miraculously produced enough wine to render at least 1,024 people unfit to drive a donkey cart. At least by today's measure of intoxication.

Some Christians would bristle at that, and argue that the "wine" was tasty grape juice or diluted into grape-flavored water.

Other Christians would raise a glass and say, "Cheers."

91 The Bible says there's just one God. But Jesus said he's God's divine Son and there is a divine Holy Spirit, too. How could there be just one God, yet three?

This is the reason above all reasons why Jews aren't Christians. The very idea of a Trinity of gods contradicts their core teaching:

> The Lord is our God. The Lord is the one and only God.
>
> Deuteronomy 6:4 NIRV

There's one God.
Not two.
Not three.

Any Jew who worshiped Jesus or prayed to the Holy Spirit would have a second, huge hurdle to jump as well—the top commandment of the Big Ten: "Do not worship any god except me" (Exodus 20:3 CEV).

In fairness to Jews, even the Christian Bible with its New Testament add-on doesn't use the T word: *Trinity*. But most Christian Bible experts say the idea is there.

- **Baptize in three names.** "Baptize them in the name of the Father, and of the Son, and of the Holy Spirit" (Matthew 28:19).
- **Jesus is the Son of God.** One Bible writer explained why he wrote: "These miracles have been written so that you will believe that Jesus is the Messiah, the Son of God" (John 20:31).
- **Jesus and God are one.** "The Father and I are one" (John 10:30).
- **God's Spirit empowers people.** "You will receive power when the Holy Spirit comes to you" (Acts 1:8).

Here's a reason some Christians would recommend skipping any seminar that promises to explain the Trinity: No one understands it.

Even the gospel of John, written to convince people that Jesus was the Son of God, doesn't explain how there can be only one God and yet how Jesus and God are one. The writer—traditionally presumed to have been Jesus' close disciple John—simply made the statement and backed it up with reports of the godlike miracles Jesus did.

Early church scholars tried to explain the Trinity, but they eventually gave up. They admitted they didn't understand it, but they decided to believe it anyhow—because the concept is in the Bible.

Expressing the majority opinion, Ambrose (about 340–397), bishop of Milan, Italy, wrote, "We don't confuse Father, Son, and Holy Spirit with each other. Instead, we believe they are distinct. We don't understand the mystery of how this can be, or what causes it. But we trust the evidence of this truth."

92 Paul and other Christians in the early church spoke in "heavenly languages." Why do most churches not allow it in their worship services, when it is clearly taught in the Bible?

In the Bible, "speaking in tongues," as it's often called, refers to people who speak in either:

- **Foreign languages they have never learned:** "Believers were filled with the Holy Spirit and began to speak in other languages as the Spirit gave them the ability to speak" (Acts 2:4–6).
- **Heavenly languages that sound like gibberish to most people:** "If you have the ability to speak in tongues, you will be talking only to God, since people won't be able to understand you" (1 Corinthians 14:2 NLT).

There are three main reasons many pastors say they don't want their worship services punctuated with people speaking in tongues:

- It disrupts the service.
- It's easy to fake, in a ploy to get attention.
- Visitors might think the congregation is from outer space or Kazakhstan.

Even the apostle Paul recognized the problem:

Suppose the whole congregation gathers in the same place and you speak in other languages. When outsiders or unbelievers come in, won't they say that you're out of your mind?

1 Corinthians 14:23

Paul suggested a fix, intending to limit the disruptions during worship services without totally eliminating tongues speaking:

> If people speak in other languages, only two or three at the most should speak. They should do it one at a time, and someone must interpret what each person says. But if an interpreter isn't present, those people should remain silent in church.
>
> 1 Corinthians 14:27–28

Yet even if there's an interpreter present, many pastors ask their people not to speak in tongues during worship services.

Pentecostal pastors are often an exception to the rule. Many Pentecostal churches teach that speaking in tongues is evidence that the speaker has been filled with the Holy Spirit.

That idea comes from Bible stories. For example, the household of a Roman soldier named Cornelius spoke in tongues. This convinced the apostle Peter and his companions they had been filled with the Holy Spirit: "For they [Peter and friends] heard them speaking in tongues" (Acts 10:46 NIV).

93 Paul said, "Women will be saved through childbearing." Not saved by Jesus? What about women who can't have children? Or those who took Paul's advice not to get married?

Yeah, that sounds like Paul is flip-flopping. He seems to tell Timothy one thing: women need to have kids to get saved (1 Timothy 2:15). But he tells the church in Corinth another: it's best if women don't get married (1 Corinthians 7:8).

217

We're reading both of these odd statements pulled out of a couple of letters Paul wrote. And we don't know much about the context. So Bible scholars have to guess.

Saved through childbearing. Bible experts say Paul was probably pushing back against an anti-marriage heresy he wrote about in the same letter to Timothy: "These liars . . . will tell you not to get married. They'll tell you not to eat this or that food—perfectly good food" (1 Timothy 4:2–3 THE MESSAGE).

If this educated guess is right, Paul was saying Christians should run away from that self-denial brand of Christianity and that it's okay for women to get married and have kids—God will save mothers, too.

Stay single. That educated guess about getting married seems odd when it's slapped next to Paul's advice for people to stay single—like he is.

Scholars say Paul wrote this letter to Christians in Corinth, Greece, perhaps a decade before he wrote that "saved through childbearing" letter to Timothy.

That would put it early in Paul's ministry, when many scholars say Paul mistakenly thought Jesus would return any moment: "We who are still alive will be taken in the clouds to meet the Lord in the air" (1 Thessalonians 4:17).

Paul may have had several reasons for puffing up singlehood:

- **The clock is ticking.** So little time to save souls, but so many souls to save.

- **No diapers to change.** A single person has more time to devote to ministry than a person who has to shoo kids off to school and help her husband get the remote back from the dog.

- **It's simpler.** See above. "Sometimes I wish everyone were single like me—a simpler life in many ways!" (1 Corinthians 7:7 THE MESSAGE).

94 Who should we believe? God, who said in the Old Testament, "an eye for an eye and a tooth for a tooth," or Jesus, who said in the New, "turn the other cheek"?

It looks like the Bible gives us two choices:

• Retaliate, but don't overdo it—an eye for an eye (Leviticus 24:19–20).
• Don't retaliate—turn the other cheek (Matthew 5:39).

Many scholars say that neither law was intended to be taken literally—and that the principle behind them is similar: don't let a spirit of retaliation get the better of you.

By the time of Moses, 1400s BC or 1200s BC (debated), the "eye for an eye" law was already well known throughout the ancient Middle East. And had been for several centuries.

One version of the law shows up as number 196 on a stone pillar that contains the law code of Babylon's legendary king, Hammurabi (about 1795–1750 BC): "If a man put out the eye of another man, his eye shall be put out."

Without laws like this, it would be easy for a vengeful relative to kill another person in retaliation—possibly starting a bloody feud between two families or tribes.

When it came to the Jews, some scholars say, this eye-for-an-eye law didn't give an eye-poked victim blanket permission to poke the poker. Scholars say Moses was establishing a law code to guide judges in settling disputes. Judges likely had the option of ordering offenders to pay fines.

Scholars say that's implied by two laws:

- "Never accept a cash payment in exchange for the life of a convicted murderer" (Numbers 35:31). But apparently it's okay for lesser offenses.
- "If you do something wrong to another person . . . you must confess your sin, pay in full for what you did wrong, add one-fifth to it, and give it to the person who was wronged" (Numbers 5:6–7).

Jesus took the law of limited retaliation to the next level: forgiveness.

He suggested that instead of nurturing a spirit of justice when it comes to people who have hurt us, we'd be better off if we nurtured a spirit of forgiveness.

That certainly doesn't come naturally. We want justice.

Yet many Christians would argue that the sooner we can forgive, the sooner we can get on with our lives.

Perhaps one way to observe both laws at the same time would be to seek justice for others we know have been exploited or hurt, but to offer forgiveness when we're the ones who have been hurt.

95 God ordered murderers executed. So when Cain killed Abel, and when David had Bathsheba's husband killed, why did God let them go?

Never murder" (Exodus 20:13). It's one of the Top Ten Commandments.

According to the laws of Moses, a convicted, cold-blooded killer had just one option—drop dead: "Never accept a cash payment in exchange for the life of a convicted murderer who has been given the death penalty. Murderers must be put to death" (Numbers 35:31). Moses explained why the killer had to be killed: "Murder pollutes the land. Only one thing can pay to remove the pollution in the land where murder has been committed. The blood of the one who spilled another's blood must be spilled" (Numbers 35:33 NIRV). Cain and David were both murderers. No doubt about it.

- "Cain attacked his brother Abel and killed him" (Genesis 4:8).
- "David wrote a letter to Joab [an army commander]. . . . 'Put Uriah on the front line where the fighting is heaviest. Then abandon him so that he'll be struck down and die'" (2 Samuel 11:14–15).

If God had lived by the laws that Moses said God gave him, Cain and David would have been executed. Why they weren't is just one question among thousands in the Bible that remain unanswered.

Students of the Bible offer a few speculative comments and theories:

- Cain's story was just a legend. There was no murder.
- Moses wrote the laws himself but said they came from God.
- God wrote the laws but had his reasons for not always enforcing them. He doesn't need to explain his reasons to us.
- If Cain had died, the world would have missed his sons: Jabal, "the first person to live in tents and have livestock"; Jubal, "the first person to play the harp and the flute"; and Tubal-cain, "who made bronze and iron tools," the first metalworker (Genesis 4:20–22).
- If David had died, Israel's borders might not have been secured and Solomon would never have been born.
- If Solomon had never been born to David and Bathsheba, David's family tree would never have made it to Jesus: "This is the list of ancestors of Jesus Christ. . . . David and Uriah's

wife Bathsheba were the father and mother of Solomon" (Matthew 1:1, 6).

In short, many would argue, there are rules and there are exceptions to the rules. God and wise judges know when to enforce the rules and when to bend them.

 96 Why do so many Christians try to impose their beliefs about abortion on those who don't agree with them? The Bible says absolutely nothing about abortion.

M ost Christians seem to read abortion into one of the Top Ten Commandments: "Never murder" (Exodus 20:13). That makes it a big deal.

The Roman Catholic Church opposes abortion in all cases unless the mother's life is at risk. Even then, the church describes abortion as both good and bad: Good because it saves a life. Bad because it takes a life.

Yet many other Christians say they don't make the link between abortion and murder. They argue that every case of murder reported in the Bible involves a breathing human being.

Never a fetus.

Why some Christians allow abortion

Many Christians say the decision about whether or not to abort a fetus is best left to the woman and her doctor. Among their arguments:

Abortion isn't mentioned in the Bible. Yet abortion was taking place at the time:

- "With drugs . . . midwives can . . . cause miscarriage if they so decide" (Socrates, 469–399 BC, quoted in Plato's *Theaetetus*).
- "When couples have children in excess, let abortion be procured before sense and life have begun" (Aristotle, about 384–322 BC, writing in *Politics*).

If Jesus or anyone else in Bible times considered abortion a sin, they should have said so. That's the take of some Christians. And if it is as wrong as murder, these Christians add, wouldn't they have said so?

The Bible verses some Christians cite to oppose abortion (see below), are usually excerpts from poetry taken out of context. The poets were thanking God for taking care of them. Abortion wasn't on their mind, scholars say.

Without a clear statement that abortion is sinful, some Christians say we shouldn't presume it is. And we certainly shouldn't unload that dump truck of guilt onto a woman dealing with a crisis pregnancy.

***Fetus* and *human* aren't equal in the Bible.** If a man killed a pregnant woman, he was executed. But if he caused her only to miscarry, he paid a fine:

> When there's a fight and in the fight a pregnant woman is hit so that she miscarries but is not otherwise hurt, the one responsible has to pay whatever the husband demands in compensation. But if there is further damage, then you must give life for life.
>
> Exodus 21:22–23 THE MESSAGE

Some Bible translations substitute *premature birth* for *miscarries*. But *miscarriage* tracks with similar laws from Hammurabi's Code (209–210), written in what is now Iraq, several hundred years before Moses delivered God's laws to the Jews.

Hammurabi demanded execution for injury causing death, but only a fine of ten silver coins for injury causing a miscarriage.

Jewish priests conducted a ritual to induce abortion. Women suspected of adultery had to endure a religious ritual sometimes called the Test of the Bitter Water. They drank water mixed with dirt from the worship center's floor. If a woman was guilty, "the water that brings a curse and causes bitter suffering . . . will enter her, her abdomen will swell and her womb will miscarry" (Numbers 5:27 NIV).

The literal phrase for *miscarry* is "her thigh will waste away." Other Bible translations:

- "Her uterus will drop."
- "It will make her body unable to have children" (NIRV).
- "Her womb shall discharge, her uterus drop" (NRSV).

It's unknown when life begins. The Bible never says when God places a soul into a body, making that person truly human.

In Genesis, it seems to have been when Adam took his first breath: "The Lord God . . . blew the breath of life into his nostrils. The man became a living being" (Genesis 2:7).

Christians should help women in crisis. Women in a crisis pregnancy need support. Instead, what they often get from Christians is guilt based on Bible laws that are merely presumed and not always stated clearly.

If a woman gives in to those demands and delivers the child she doesn't want, she is suddenly abandoned by those Christians. That's a charge made by some folks sympathetic to women in crisis pregnancies.

Those who discourage a woman in poverty or in college from having an abortion, for example, usually don't offer financial help in raising the child—when finances may have been the very reason the woman wanted to delay having children.

For this reason, some pro-choice Christians say pro-life Christians should put up or shut up.

Why many Christians oppose abortion

Life is sacred. All Christians agree on that.

But many Christians say the abortion of a fetus is exactly the same as killing a breathing human being.

Here are some of the arguments made by Christians who oppose abortion:

The unborn are important to God. They say that seems clear in the Bible:

- "You created my body from a tiny drop" (Job 10:10 CEV).
- "You knitted me together inside my mother" (Psalm 139:13).

Life begins inside the uterus, long before birth.

- "You knitted me together inside my mother. . . . Your eyes saw me when I was only a fetus. Every day of my life was recorded in your book before one of them had taken place" (Psalm 139:13, 16).

The early church opposed abortion. Though abortion might not be mentioned specifically in the Bible, it shows up in the early church manuals and in the writings of church leaders:

- "You should not murder a child by abortion" (*Didache*, first known Christian manual, AD 100s).
- "There is no difference between killing a life that has already been born or one that is in the process of birth" (Tertullian, Christian scholar, about AD 160–225).
- "The rich kill the fruit of their own bodies in the womb so their inheritance isn't spread thin, destroying their own children in the womb with murderous poisons" (St. Ambrose, Italian bishop, about AD 339–397).

Watch the video. For some Christians who oppose abortion, the strongest evidence against it isn't in the Bible. It's in science.

Though most abortions are performed before viability—before the child could live on its own outside the womb—many Christians insist that life is well on its way by the time of the abortion.

According to the Mayo Clinic, the unborn child shows the following characteristics at the various stages of development:

- **Week 6.** Basic facial features begin to appear. Buds develop that will become arms and legs.
- **Week 7.** Brain and face are developing rapidly. Tiny nostrils become visible. Eye lenses begin to form.
- **Week 8.** Arms and legs grow longer. Eyes are visible. Ears are forming. Upper lip and nose have formed.
- **Week 9.** Bones form and there is a bend at the elbows. Toes form. Baby is about three quarters of an inch long—about the size of a kidney bean.

Watching a video of an abortion procedure gives a visual of exactly what is being destroyed. Many Christians opposed to abortion say they believe that if women knew more about what is inside them, they would decide against abortion.

Christians should help the helpless. There's no one on earth more helpless than an unborn child, many insist.

- "You're here to defend the defenseless/the weak and the fatherless" (Psalm 82:3 THE MESSAGE/NIV).
- "Blessed is the one who has concern for helpless people" (Psalm 41:1).

Consider adoption. If a woman in a crisis pregnancy doesn't want the child, there are infertile couples lined up waiting for a baby to love and to raise as their own.

Christian adoption services throughout the country are on a mission as nonprofit agencies whose primary purpose is to match children with loving, Christ-centered families.

Abortion is a volatile topic among Christians. Life-or-death stuff. All good Christians want to help.
The disagreement erupts over the matter of who to help:

- the unborn child
- the woman who doesn't want the child growing inside her own body.

97 Why do Christians think Jesus is unique when ancient religions are full of stories about supposed gods or leaders being born of a virgin or under a special star, performing miracles, and even rising from the dead?

It's true, there are plenty of legends about gods and humans that sound like the writers borrowed a few pages from the story of Jesus. Or, worse, that the Bible writers borrowed a few pages from Middle Eastern legends.

Legends

Virgin birth. An Egyptian legend from centuries before Jesus says that Isis, the great mother goddess, conceived Horus, the hawk-headed god of war, without having sexual relations.

Raised from the dead. Egyptian legends also claim Isis raised her god-husband, Osiris, from the dead after his brother murdered him and chopped him to bits.

Born under starlight. A Greek legend says that Alexander the Great—conqueror of most of the ancient Middle East, all the way to India—was destined for greatness because he was born on the night of a bright constellation.

Miracles galore. One Muslim legend claims God split the moon to convince a group of people that Muhammad was a prophet.

Buddha (about 500 BC) was said to have performed the "Twin Miracle" to prove he was really enlightened when some doubted him. His upper body produced flames and his lower body produced streams of water. Then he shifted this phenomenon to his right side and left side. Also, during a flood, Buddha is said to have parted the water so he could walk on dry ground.

Jesus is unique

The stories of Jesus are unique for several reasons.

Roman history. For one, the story of his resurrection shows up in a first-century Roman history book:

> There was a wise man called Jesus, and his conduct was good. . . . Pilate condemned him to be crucified. . . . His disciples didn't abandon their loyalty to him. They reported that he appeared to them three days after his crucifixion, and that he was alive.
>
> Josephus (c. AD 37–101), *Antiquities of the Jews*

Disciple martyrs. The Bible and early church writings confirm that Jesus' original disciples were utterly convinced that he died and rose again—and that they would rise again, too. They were so convinced that almost all of them died telling people about the life, teachings, and resurrection of Jesus.

Even many Jewish scholars today say it's obvious that the disciples were convinced of the resurrection, though most Jews don't seem convinced that the disciples actually saw what they said they saw.

Miracles to fuel a movement. What's also unique about the story of Jesus is that the Christian movement drew its energy from the story of his resurrection, along with miracles the disciples produced to back up the story.

A little over a month after Jewish leaders orchestrated Jesus' execution in Jerusalem, the Bible says the Holy Spirit filled the disciples, who had been in hiding. Apparently, they were afraid they might be executed, as well.

"All the believers were filled with the Holy Spirit and began to speak in other languages as the Spirit gave them the ability to speak" (Acts 2:4).

They marched boldly into the streets—in front of the very Jewish leaders who had condemned Jesus to death—and began telling people about Jesus and what had happened.

The city was crammed full of Jewish pilgrims from all over the Middle East. They had come for the May harvest festival of Shavuot. And they each heard the disciples "speaking in [their] native dialects" (Acts 2:8).

A crowd formed. Peter preached. And about 3,000 Jews joined the messianic movement that became known as The Way, and later as Christianity.

Miracles of healing throughout Jerusalem convinced many others. By this time, Christianity was unstoppable. It proved ineffective to threaten these early Christians with execution for heresy, as the Jews did, or for practicing an outlawed religion, as the Romans did. These Christians believed that just as Jesus rose from the dead to live forever, they would follow in his celestial footprints.

If a spiritual body leaves footprints.

229

98 Why do Christians insist that Jesus is predicted in the Jewish Bible, when Jews don't seem to see him there?

Here are a few of the Old Testament prophecies that many Christians say identify Jesus as the Messiah the Jews had been waiting for.

Prophecy	Christian view of fulfillment	Jewish views
Virgin birth. "The Lord himself will give you this sign: A virgin will become pregnant and give birth to a son, and she will name him Immanuel [God Is With Us]" (Isaiah 7:14).	**Virgin Mary.** "You will become pregnant, give birth to a son, and name him Jesus. . . . Mary asked the angel, 'How can this be? I've never had sexual intercourse.' The angel answered her, 'The Holy Spirit will come to you, and the power of the Most High will overshadow you. Therefore, the holy child developing inside you will be called the Son of God'" (Luke 1:31, 34–35).	**Wrong century, wrong woman.** Isaiah was talking to his king, 700 years before Jesus. Isaiah promised that God would kill their enemies before a certain young woman— not necessarily a virgin—would have a child and the child would be able to tell right from wrong. (See Question 72, "Why do Christians say the prophet Isaiah predicted . . . Jesus 700 years ahead of time?")
Born in Bethlehem. "You, Bethlehem Ephrathah, are too small to be included among Judah's cities. Yet, from you Israel's future ruler will come for me" (Micah 5:2).	**Jesus' birth town.** "The Savior—yes, the Messiah, the Lord—has been born today in Bethlehem" (Luke 2:11 NLT).	**Big deal.** Lots of people were born in Bethlehem.

Prophecy	Christian view of fulfillment	Jewish views
King on a donkey. "Shout in triumph, people of Jerusalem! Look! Your King is coming to you: He is righteous and victorious. He is humble and rides on a donkey" (Zechariah 9:9).	**Jesus on a donkey.** "They brought the donkey to Jesus. . . . As he was riding along, people spread their coats on the road [to Jerusalem]. . . . They shouted joyfully, 'Blessed is the king who comes in the name of the Lord!'" (Luke 19:35–38).	**Manufactured.** Jesus knew his Bible. He choreographed this by renting the donkey and sending his disciples to get it for him: "You will find a young donkey tied there" (Luke 19:30).
Suffering servant. "The Lord laid on him the sins of us all. . . . He was led like a lamb to the slaughter. . . . He had done no wrong. . . . He was buried like a criminal; he was put in a rich man's grave" (Isaiah 53:6–7, 9 NLT).	**Jesus crucified.** "The Son of Man . . . came . . . to give his life as a ransom for many." He was buried in the tomb of a rich Jew: Joseph of Arimathea (Mark 10:45; Mark 15:43).	**Israel is the servant.** The prophecy symbolizes the Jewish people and the unjust suffering they experienced during exile in what is now Iraq during the 500s BC.
Feeling deserted. "My God, my God, why have you abandoned me?" (Psalm 22:1).	**Jesus feeling deserted.** On the cross Jesus seems to quote that psalm: "My God, my God, why have you abandoned me?" (Matthew 27:46). The psalm ends thanking God for salvation: "he has finished it" (Psalm 22:31). Those were Jesus' last words: "It is finished!" (John 19:30).	**Nice quote.** Jesus may well have believed—even to his dying breath—that he was the Messiah and God's Son. But the Jewish Bible says nothing about God having a son.
Resurrected on third day. "After two days he will revive us. On the third day he will raise us so that we may live in his presence" (Hosea 6:2).	**Day 3, Jesus resurrected.** "People hung him on a cross and killed him, but God brought him back to life on the third day" (Acts 10:39–40).	**Don't take poetry literally.** Hosea, warning about the coming fall of Israel, was assuring the Jews that God would restore their nation—but that it would take time.

99 Even if there is a heaven and hell, why do Christians obsess over it? Hasn't God already decided who goes where?

The Bible says no such thing.

Not according to how lots of Christians read the Bible. Here's the problem: The library of books that make up the Bible sends mixed messages about whether God

- tells us where to go
- lets us make up our own mind about it

Many Bible scholars admit that the signals are mixed.

Evidence of mixed signals: Christians tend to park their beliefs in one of two camps: the sovereignty of God or man's free will.

Sovereignty of God

He's the boss. He decides who will get saved and who won't (tech term: predestination).

Theological father: John Calvin (1509–1564), France

Churches that buy into the idea: many Baptist, Presbyterian, and churches with *Reformed* in the name

Go-to Bible passages, followed by "Free will" Christian counterpoints:

- "Those God foreknew he also predestined to be conformed to the image of his Son. . . . And those he predestined, he also called; those he called, he also justified" (Romans 8:29–30 NIV).

Counterpoint: Instead of *predestined*, read *chose* or *planned*. That's how many Bibles translate it. God chooses to save everyone—and created a plan to make it happen. But not everyone chooses to let him save them. God knows who will choose him, but we're the ones making the call. Knowing what we're going to do isn't the same as making us do it. We control our own spiritual destiny, even if God knows what we'll do.

- "Before the creation of the world, he chose us through Christ to be holy and perfect in his presence. Because of his love he had already decided to adopt us through Jesus Christ" (Ephesians 1:4–5).

  Counterpoint: God chose everyone. He wants everyone to be his holy children, adopted through Christ.

- "People cannot come to me [Jesus] unless the Father who sent me brings them to me" (John 6:44).

  Counterpoint: God points everyone to Jesus and the salvation he offers.

Free will among humans

We're the boss of our spiritual destiny. We decide whether or not to follow the teachings of Jesus.

Theological father: John Wesley (1703–1791), England

Churches that buy into the idea: Methodist, Freewill Baptist, Church of the Nazarene, Salvation Army

Go-to Bible passages, followed by "sovereignty" Christian counterpoints:

- "God wants everyone to be saved" (1 Timothy 2:4 CEV).

  Counterpoint: God wants all people to turn from evil, but he empowers only certain people.

- "God loved the world so much that he gave his one and only Son. Anyone who believes in him will not die but will have eternal life" (John 3:16 NIRV).

    Counterpoint: The only ones who will believe are the ones God chose.

- "The Lord . . . doesn't want to destroy anyone but wants all people to have an opportunity to turn to him and change the way they think and act" (2 Peter 3:9).

    Counterpoint: Peter was talking only about those who are chosen by God.

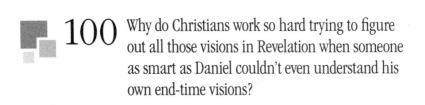

100 Why do Christians work so hard trying to figure out all those visions in Revelation when someone as smart as Daniel couldn't even understand his own end-time visions?

It's true enough. The angel Gabriel had to explain Daniel's vision to him: "As I, Daniel, was trying to understand the meaning of this vision, someone who looked like a man stood in front of me. And I heard a human voice calling out . . . 'Gabriel, tell this man the meaning of his vision'" (Daniel 8:15–16 NLT).

If Daniel was stumped about his own vision, where do folks today get the chutzpah to think they can interpret visions other people had thousands of years ago?

Maybe it's not so much chutzpah as it is curiosity. Most Christians want to know what's coming and when it's coming—especially if it's the end of the world.

There are plenty of writers and preachers willing to tell them—for the love of God or the love of money. Only the good Lord knows which.

We can't know the motives of people who say they've figured out a prophecy. All we can know for certain is that some folks have made a pile of money by feeding our end-time curiosity with predictions that never came true.

- Hal Lindsey, a campus chaplain who sold 35 million copies of a book that predicted Jesus would come within one generation of Israel's becoming a nation. Israel became a nation in 1948—approaching two generations ago.
- Edgar Whisenant, a NASA rocket engineer who sold 4 million copies of *88 Reasons Why the Rapture Will Be in 1988*. Someone could have come up with eighty-eight reasons why it wouldn't. But who would have bought it?
- Lee Jang Rim, a South Korean minister who predicted Jesus would return in 1992, but pocketed $4 million and invested in bonds that matured in 1993. He might have thought of that as a win-win until a judge jailed him for two years.
- Jack Van Impe, a Baptist televangelist who suggested that the Mayans may have been on to something with their 2012 dead-end calendar.

Most scholars admit that one problem with interpreting Bible prophecy is that it's usually written as poetry, which is laced in symbolism. That's especially true of end-time prophecy—like Revelation. It's written in a style of poetry called apocalyptic literature, famous for its extreme and sometimes bizarre symbolism.

Take, for example, the seven-headed dragon that tried to eat a woman's newborn baby: "Her child was snatched away and taken to God and to his throne" (Revelation 12:5).

Plenty of Bible experts say the dragon represents Satan tempting Jesus. Others guess the dragon was King Herod ordering his soldiers to kill the baby boys of Bethlehem, in an effort to kill baby Jesus.

There are also lots of guesses about the mark of the beast: "The beast's number is 666" (Revelation 13:18). In some ancient Bibles the number is 616. Both numbers point nicely to Roman Emperor Nero, many scholars say.

Nero was the first emperor to persecute Christians. Some scholars explain that linking Nero to the beast is one piece of evidence suggesting that Revelation was mainly a commentary about the persecution of Christians in Roman times.

Some Roman coins were stamped with the words *Nero Caesar*. Letters in ancient times had number values. N = 50, C = 100. When you tally the letters from the Hebrew version of these words—the language of the Jews—you get 666. When you tally the letters from the Greek version of these words—the international language of the day—you get 616.

Yet many Bible experts say there is a future beast coming, too. They back that theory up by pointing to prophecies they say have not yet been fulfilled.

Since it's so hard to piece together the mystery of end-time prophecies, and there's no way to know for certain if the picture we come up with is anywhere close to accurate, many Christians go about their business, filing the mysteries under *Pending*.

These Christians take the implied advice angels gave the disciples after Jesus ascended: "Why do you stand here looking at the sky?" (Acts 1:11 NIRV).

The disciples moved along and got busy telling the story of Jesus and doing the best they could to live the way he taught them to live: loving God and loving others.

That's how the Christian movement started.

Many would argue that's how the Christian movement lives on, from one generation to the next.

Stephen M. Miller (BA, news journalism, Kent State University; MRE, religious education, Nazarene Theological Seminary) is a full-time free-lance writer who treats the Bible as his beat. His *Who's Who and Where's Where in the Bible* won the Retailer's Choice Award as best nonfiction book of the year. *The Bible: A History* won best nonfiction book of the year in England. *How to Get Into the Bible* was a Gold Medallion finalist—one of the top five Bible study books of the year. His books have sold over a million copies.